Kundalini Awakening

*An Essential Guide to Achieving Higher
Consciousness, Opening the Third Eye,
Balancing Your Chakras, and Understanding
Spiritual Enlightenment*

Contents

Introduction

Let me start by sharing my personal experiences with you. I heard the word "Kundalini" in passing some years ago. I read about it on the Internet and then forgot about it altogether. Then, one day, suddenly as I was having a party with my friends, something strange took place.

I was introduced to a lady named June, who called herself a psychic healer. I smiled condescendingly at her when she told me she was a psychic. She smiled back and said, "Your life is not going to be the same after tomorrow." She simply walked away after making that statement to me. "Rubbish," I thought. With her comment in the back of my mind, I had a good time and went home and went to bed.

As I lay down on my bed, a sharp feeling of something rising up my spine hit me so hard that I got up in fright. I looked under the sheets to see if something had bitten me. But no! The bed and the sheets were clean. My head whirled as the sharp feeling now seemed to be in my head. My head was swimming, and I thought I was going to die. I was alone at home and remember feeling panicked.

The closest thing that came to mind for support was a glass of wine. I poured myself a small quantity and sat on the couch in front of the TV. My daughter had gone for a class picnic, and somehow and inexplicably, I knew I had to reach out to her. I called her on the phone, and she said that her camp was in the middle of a huge landslide! I quickly called my friend who lived close to the camp, and within minutes my daughter and some of her friends were picked up and brought home to safety!

I was relieved, but the uncanny experience left me shaken. How did I know I had to call my daughter at that time? What was the feeling I had of something sharp and painful rushing up my spine? Why did I feel like I was not alone and there were people with me in the room? It was weird and scary.

The next morning, I called June. She became my mentor and guided me on my journey of Kundalini Awakening. She told me that what I had experienced the night before was rooted in ancient teachings. I remembered reading about it a few years before. June said that the reading I did years ago was the first spark ready to become a full-blown fire now.

With her help, I learned to navigate through the journey of Kundalini Awakening. I learned about the different subtopics and how to awaken this strange power, and yet, keep it under my control. I learned about tantra, mantra, kriyas, yoga, asanas, meditation techniques, Shakti, Shiva, and much more. This book is a collection of all my lessons of Kundalini and its awakening process.

This practical guide to Kundalini Awakening helps novices understand the limitless power that each of us holds in our beings and teaches you how you can unleash it and use it for your own good and for the good of the people around you.

Chapter 1: The Very Basics: Kundalini, Shakti and Prana

According to Hinduism, *Kundalini* is defined as the divine feminine energy lying latent at the base of the spine (which is called the Muladhara) in the form of a coiled snake. Kundalini is a Sanskrit word that translates to a "coiled snake."

Shaiva Tantra, a tantric subsect of Hinduism, also believes in the deep power of Kundalini. According to Shaiva Tantra, the power of the Adi Parashakti or Mahadevi, the supreme feminine deity, lies in a latent dormant state as a coiled snake in the Muladhara. Other names of Adi Parashakti are:

- Parama Shakti
- Adi Shakti
- Mahashakti
- Mahadevi
- Mahagauri
- Mahakali
- Satyam Shakti

In Sanskrit, Parama means "absolute," "maha" means "great," and Satya means "truth." This powerful female deity is also simply referred to as "Shakti." The Kundalini is also associated with other female deities such as Kubjika and Bhairavi.

In the 9th century, the concepts based on Kundalini Shakti were incorporated into Hatha Yoga. Hatha in Sanskrit translates to "force," which refers to a practice that focuses on physical techniques. Today, Kundalini concepts have been introduced into many other forms of Hinduism and New Age Philosophical thoughts of the western world.

Waking up the coiled snake at the Muladhara is the basis of Kundalini awakening. Ancient traditions speak of different methods, including Tantra, Mantra, Yantra, and Asanas, or meditation that can be used for Kundalini awakening.

Tantra refers to an esoteric tradition that developed almost simultaneously both from Buddhism and Hinduism around the middle of the first millennium. Mantra refers to the system of chanting sacred sounds in the form of syllables, words or groups of words, or even verses.

Yantra (known to be rooted in Tantra) refers to the system of drawing intricate mystical diagrams used for prayer and worship. These diagrams are to be used in meditation and they are believed to have occult powers that can be harnessed to benefit the practitioner. Asanas are body postures originally used for meditation but later on introduced into Hatha Yoga as a form of physical exercise. According to the Yoga Sutras of Patanjali, an asana is defined as a position you can hold for some time, comfortably and stably.

Meditation involves using various techniques to train the mind to focus on an object or thought or any other tool to achieve a calm and stable state. These Kundalini awakening methods are discussed in another chapter. Kundalini Yoga is highly influenced by Shaktism and various Tantra schools of Hinduism. The state of Kundalini Awakening is often described as a distinct, clear feeling of electric current passing through the spine.

Etymology of Kundalini

Kundalini Yoga or Kundalini Shakti is found in the ancient Hindu scriptures called the Upanishads. These are believed to have been formulated anywhere between the 7th and the 9th century BC, or perhaps even before. The dates are irrelevant for the study of the esoteric but wonderful subject of Kundalini, except to know that it is an ancient practice used by humankind for centuries.

The root of the word "Kundalini" is in the Sanskrit verb, "kindalin," which means "annular or circular." The word is mentioned as a noun for a snake in a coiled position in a work of the 12th century called Rajatarangini. This was a chronicle of the kings and kingdoms of the area that forms part of present-day Northern India.

"Kunda," which is a Sanskrit name for water-pot or bowl, is the name of a Naga (a serpent character) in the Mahabharata, one of two epics of Hinduism, the other being Ramayan. Mahabharata is also believed to have been composed in the centuries before the birth of Christ.

In Shaktism and Tantrism, "kundali" is often used as a name of Goddess Durga, another form of Shakti from the 11th century onward. During the 15th century, Kundalini was adopted into Hatha Yoga as a technical term, and the practice of Kundalini awakening began to be practiced widely around the 16th century. Kundalini can, therefore, be rephrased as 'the coiled power" that lies dormant at the base of the spine.

Tantric Shaivism and the Kundalini

Shaivism (dates to the 5th century) or Shaiva Siddhanta (which translates to 'the doctrine of Shiva") is the oldest known tradition of Tantric Shaivism. Shaivism emphasizes devotion to and worship of Lord Shiva, who is believed to be the supreme being of the universe. The theology of Shaivism presents three universal realities, namely:

- The pashu (or the individual soul of every human)
- The pati (or the Supreme Being which is Lord Shiva)
- The Pasha (which represents the soul's bondage and attachment to the materialistic world because of ignorance (the lack of ultimate spiritual knowledge), karma (our actions in the materialistic world), and Maya (the inability to see beyond the illusion of materialism)

Shaivism propagates community service, ethical living and commitment to one's profession, loving devotion to Lord Shiva, yoga practice, and continuous building of self-awareness as important tenets for the liberation of individual souls. Some experts believe that Shaiva Tantra could have originated in Kashmir around the 10th century. However, after Islamic invasions in the north, Shaivism propagated more in the southern parts of India. Besides India, Shaiva Siddhanta is popular in other countries such as Singapore, Malaysia, and Sri Lanka.

Kundalini is a principal tenet in Shaktism, a cult within the Shaiva tradition. Followers of Shaktism believe that the all-encompassing metaphysical reality is in the feminine energy, Shakti, who is the Supreme Godhead. The Kundalini represents this innate and all-pervading metaphysical consciousness.

A visual image of the coiled snake is mentioned in an 8th-century Tantric text called Tantra Sadbhava-tantra. In this description, Shakti is the central channel, and the life force or the prana moves in the upward direction. This upward movement of the Kundalini Shakti from the base of the spine has been referred to in many later works.

In Shaktism, the Kundalini is the latent innate spiritual power, a representation of Goddess Kubjika, or the "Crooked One," who is also known as Paradevi or the Supreme Goddess. Paradevi is also the ultimate source of all power and pure bliss. She is the source of all mantras. She resides in the six chakras (a separate chapter in this book deals with the chakras in detail) along the central channel.

Tantric traditions also talk about two types of Kundalini. One is the upward moving type of Kundalini (or the urdhva), which is connected with expansion and growth. The other is the downward moving type (or the adha), which is linked to contraction. Kundalini, therefore, is the power to manifest body, breath, and the experiences of pleasure and pain. It uses sexuality as the source of reproduction.

The Awakening of the Kundalini

The awakening of the Kundalini is described as the progress the innate spiritual energy makes as it rises from the base of the spine or Muladhara to move upwards toward the top of the head. During Kundalini Awakening, the vibration of the practitioner suddenly skips levels.

As the innate spiritual energy or vibration passes through the various chakras on its way to the top, the practitioner experiences different levels of awakening combined with a mystical experience at each chakra. When this innate spiritual energy reaches the top of the head or the Sahasrara (or the crown chakra), the practitioner is believed to experience a profound transformation of consciousness.

Sages and rishis who have had this profound experience have left awe-inspiring descriptions for the layman to read. Swami Shivananda Saraswati of the Divine Life Society has recorded his experience in his book titled Kundalini Yoga. He writes, "*When the crown chakra is breached, the practitioner will experience supersensual visions in his or her mental eye. He or she can experience new worlds filled with indescribable charms and wonders. The practitioner can see new and hitherto hidden planes of consciousness. The yogi will experience pure bliss, power, knowledge, and more in increasing degrees, unheard of in the human world.*"

More About Shakti

According to Shaktism, Shakti, or Prana, is the ultimate source of everything in this universe. Everything you see around you, and feel and experience within you, are just various manifestations of this all-encompassing Shakti. Shakti pervades everything here and is far subtler and finer than the finest quanta of energy measurable within the tangible, physical universe we humans can sense or feel.

The power of Shakti, or Prana, can be ignored in the normal world or by people not looking to harness its deeper capabilities. However, it is possible for those who are willing to draw it out, work with it, mobilize and direct it, and even use it as a force. Experienced practitioners of Kundalini Yoga know that it is possible to harness and use the power of the innate, latent Shakti or Prana just as we use and harness the power of electricity.

When we breach the power of Kundalini Shakti, we will be subject to and surrender to the universal power that facilitates new experiences beyond realms imagined by humans. Practitioners warn novices not to reach out to the power of Shakti or Prana unless your body and mind are in good shape and you are completely tuned in to the higher energy frequencies.

There are multiple cases of novices returning, completely shaken and paranoid after experiencing the higher potential of Shakti or prana that lies latent and dormant in Muladhara in the form of Kundalini. If you try to do something you are not ready for, it is like trying to put 220 volts of power into a socket with a capacity of withstanding only 110 V.

There is a process of purification of the mind, body, and soul you have to complete before you can try to achieve those high energy levels. This process of purification helps your body, mind, and soul to become containers that can handle far more love and compassion than they can presently hold and connect with. Your mind has to learn to be quieter, and your body has to become stronger, and your heart has to be more open to fully harness the potential of Shakti.

As mentioned earlier, a Kundalini Awakening can be described as akin to when our energy vibrations skip levels and move up. To give you an analogy, in school, we go from Grade 1 to Grade 2 to Grade 3, and so forth in well-defined steps, right? Now, imagine you could skip a couple of grades and go from Grade 4 straight to Grade 7. What would happen?

Your body and mind are exposed to the life of a Grade 7 who is not yet ready to accept the challenges of this grade because he or she hasn't yet learned what was taught in Grade 5 and 6. Interestingly, skipping of vibration levels can happen for multiple reasons, including physical and emotional trauma, emotional outbursts, deep meditation, etc. When you practice structured methods defined and designed for the Kundalini awakenings, then you are essentially preparing yourself to receive its power.

More About Prana

The Sanskrit word "prana" means "vital life force." Other meanings of this wide-ranging powerful word include 'the breath of life," "vital air," "principle of life," and so forth. In Hindu texts, prana is sometimes described as originating from the Sun and is believed to connect all the elements.

The concept of prana or the vital life force is described in ancient Hindu texts, including the Upanishads and the Vedas. This concept is explained in great detail in the literature of Hatha Yoga, Ayurveda (Indian medicine), and Tantra systems. The prana is typically divided into five components, namely:

> ➢ Prana (or the inward moving energy)

> ➢ Apana (the outward moving energy)

> ➢ Vyana (the circulation of energy)

> ➢ Udana (energy of the throat and head)

> Samana (energy of digestion and assimilation)

Another way of categorizing prana is through using "Vayu" which is Sanskrit for wind or air. Prana is considered the most primary and basic Vayu. All other types of Vayus emerge from Prana. So, the five components can be re-described using Vayu:

- Prana Vayu - the location of prana Vayu is considered to be the heart. It is responsible for talking, singing, laughing, fighting, dancing, art and craft, and other tasks humans do.

- Apana Vayu (the downward breath) - Located at the anus, the apana Vayu is responsible for allowing food and drink into the body, moving the waste product downwards, and finally out of the body.

- Udana Vayu (the upward breath) - Located in the throat, the Udana Vayu is responsible for coughing, hiccupping, sneezing, and vomiting.

- Samana Vayu - located at the navel, this Vayu mixes and assimilates everything that is eaten and drank.

- Vyana Vayu - Located in all the joints, this Vayu is responsible for the sense of touch, bending and movement of limbs, stomach aches, and sweating.

Hindu texts describe prana as flowing through nadis (or channels) in the body. There are multiple nadis in the human body, of which the three most important ones include:

- Ida on the left side of the body
- Pingala on the right side of the body
- Sushumna is the center that connects the Muladhara or the base chakra, to the Sahasrara or the crown chakra

Pranayama

Using various techniques to accumulate, expand and work with the prana is called pranayama. Pranayama is one of the eight methods of

Yoga practice and refers to the practice of breath control techniques. The systematic practice of pranayama allows the practitioner to gain control of the prana.

Pranayama techniques also help to cleanse the nadis and get rid of blockages in them for improved and better circulation of prana. In some traditions, pranayama is used to arrest the breath to achieve "samadhi" to bring increased awareness in any one particular part of the body. In Indian medicine or Ayurveda, pranayama is used to treat illnesses and maintenance of general health. According to Patanjali's Yoga Shastras, the ultimate goal of pranayama is the slow cessation of breath, to discontinue inhalation and exhalation in order to understand the all-pervading Supreme soul.

Difference Between Kundalini Energy (or Shakti) and Prana

At this stage, it might make sense to try to understand the differences between Kundalini Shakti (or energy) and Prana, both of which are forms of energy, and yet are different. After all, *energy* is such a common term used to describe a variety of forces. Knowing the difference between Kundalini energy and pranic energy will help you step up to the next level of spiritual development.

The energy is known by different names at various levels. For a spiritual seeker, the highest level of energy is spiritual energy. At an emotional level, love is a form of energy. At a physical level, sex between two partners is a manifestation of energy. Kundalini Awakening experiences are also a physical level of energy manifestation.

Let us start with Kundalini energy. Imagine the energy needed to create life. When a man and woman come together to create a baby, essentially, they are creating a new life, right? The sperm is considered to have a lot of potential energy in it. This is the reason when a man has an orgasm (which essentially releases millions of sperm into a small place), a lot of energy is used up.

Interestingly, sexual energy and Kundalini energy are rooted in the same place: the base of the spine. In fact, tantric practitioners can channelize their sexual energy into other parts of the body and use it for purposes other than reproduction. Try this exercise to understand what Kundalini energy is.

Squeeze your sphincter muscles (essentially the muscles of your buttocks and anus and the muscles around your stomach area) tightly as you breathe in and release the muscles as you breathe out. The exercise goes something like this:

- Squeeze in your sphincter muscles as you breathe in.
- Then hold it for 20 seconds.
- Then breathe out and release the pressure on the muscles.

Now, when holding your breath for a while, and if you are not used to holding your breath for long, you are likely to feel uncomfortable. At the stage of the discomfort, you will feel some energy rise up your spine. This energy is the same as the sexual energy that a tantric practitioner disperses to the rest of the body.

So, with the exercise involving squeezing and holding of your sphincter muscles, you are essentially trying to awaken the Kundalini Shakti or energy lying like a coiled snake at the base of your spine. The interesting thing about the awakening of the Kundalini is that not only can you experience this energy climbing in an upward direction toward your crown chakra, but also it moves in a wavelike formation, similar to the structure of the DNA.

Prana, or the pranic energy, is the universal energy that empowers everything in this universe. It connects all forms of life. Prana is also the force behind nature's workings and how everything is kept in balance. For example:

- Have you ever wondered how oxygen, carbon dioxide, the wild plants and animals, and everything else around you knows what it has to do?

- Have you ever wondered how despite lions (or other predators) killing and eating deer (or other prey), the number of prey and predators remains balanced in nature?

- Have you ever wondered how different people make up this world and live together?

- Don't you see there appears to be an ordered design behind everything in nature that keeps everything in it balanced and orderly?

The power behind this order and structure of nature is also prana or the pranic energy that pervades the entire universe. To experience the energy of the prana, try this exercise:

- Close your eyes and relax.

- Take a deep breath and then let go as much as you can.

- Repeat the deep inhalation and express as much as you can let out during the exhalation.

- As you exhale, try to let out all your emotions, thoughts and everything else you can experience. Remember, we are not trying to achieve perfection during this process. Just focus on trying to release everything out of your system as much as you can.

As you do this, try to identify that part in your body that is the source of all the energy in this universe. Yes, this place within your body, which is the source of all energy, exists. It could be anywhere. It could be in your heart, belly, chest area, head, or anywhere else. It is for you to identify this place that holds a part of the universal prana. This place in your body behaves like a reverse black hole because unlike a black hole that sucks everything in, this place fills you with infinite light.

When you find this place, try to breathe inward into this place of prana. As you do so, you will feel that all the pores in your body are opening up, and you experience the feeling of swimming in an ocean of bright, white energy that pervades and surrounds everything in and outside of you. This pranic energy nourishes your body and mind through the pineal gland and activates your body. It takes some practice to achieve these levels of focus that will get you to the place of pranic energy. However, it can be done with patient, diligent practice.

Therefore, Kundalini energy creates life, and people who experience Kundalini awakening have the power to use and disperse this Kundalini Shakti to other parts of the body. The pranic energy, on the other hand, is the source of universal power and pervades everything in the universe.

The important thing to remember about Kundalini energy is that while various methods can help you awaken it, the awakening itself can and will happen only when it is time for you. Therefore, while you practice the methods in this book, it is important not to get impatient and force anything on yourself, your body, and your mind. Instead, simply do what you have to do and wait for it to happen at the right time.

But again, is there a difference between Kundalini Energy and Pranic energy at all? Essentially, energy is the same everywhere, and only appears as different manifestations depending on the situation, place and state of mind. Therefore, in many ways, the Kundalini energy flowing through the spine is not very different from the prana flowing through it.

The prana flows through the primary channels, namely Ida (flowing up the Ida as we breathe in) and Pingala (flowing downward as we breathe out). Kundalini energy is a potentially powerful prana that lies curled up at the base of the spine. When awakened, this Kundalini energy flows up the Sushumna and has the potential to lead us to spiritual enlightenment.

Chapter 2: What is a Kundalini Awakening?

In the previous chapter, you were given a glimpse of what Kundalini Awakening can be. This chapter is dedicated entirely to Kundalini Awakening. You will learn what it is, what methods are used to awaken it (both spontaneously and consciously), the symptoms that you are likely to experience, and what it feels like.

So, to reiterate, Kundalini is the female creative energy lying latent (in the form of a coiled snake) at the base of the spine in every one of us. However, there is no physical evidence of the presence of this snake-like element in our body. It is a subtle energy form you have the power to awaken and know its presence when you experience its power.

Kundalini, like prana and the nadis or channels through which it flows, is invisible to the human eye but can be felt and experienced when it is in its active state. This subtle form of energy contains other elements of our non-physical self, including our energetic imprints, our natural and acquired patterns of energies, and emotional imprints too. Kundalini is the place where our life experiences, including the ones created by our family, culture and society (collectively called "samskara" in Sanskrit).

Interestingly, although the energy contained in our Kundalini appears metaphorical, or even metaphysical to novices, you can rest assured that it is not. Kundalini is subtle but definitely does exist and is something that many of us are capable of activating and awakening using a variety of methods, including meditation, yoga and others.

You can feel the Kundalini energy the same way you can feel your skin or see something colorful through your eyes. In the awakened state, you can feel Kundalini energy dance up and down through your spine and the nadis in your body. As it moves freely, you can also feel the dissolution of all the energy blockages in your body. As the different blockages of energy accumulated over the years are released, your insight into long-held beliefs is improved, and you can see things in a clearer form than before.

The rising up of the Kundalini is called awakening because it is literally so, the awakening from its dormant state. The Kundalini Shakti wakes up from her slumber and dances upwards in an effort to get back to Lord Shiva, the Supreme Being, according to the Shaivites. When the Kundalini Shakti breaches the crown chakra, it is like a drop of the ocean (reflecting each human) becoming one with the mighty ocean or the universal energy.

Most experts are bound to agree that awakening the Kundalini without the guidance of a guru can be dangerous, both for you and the people around you. Kundalini awakening can happen either through the conscious practice of yoga, meditation and other techniques and a result of trauma, near-death experience, a debilitating illness, in dreams, misuse, and abuse of drugs or even by having sex with a partner with an awakened Kundalini. Awakening the Kundalini requires unprecedented levels of the firm discipline of our body and mind so we can be ready to accept the responsibilities that accompany the power of waking up the innate Kundalini.

So, why should anyone try to awaken the Kundalini Shakti? Ultimately awakening the Kundalini journeys back to God or the universal divine power. It helps to get rid of your ego, too, as you surrender yourself to the universal divinity. The final purpose of Kundalini awakening is for self-realization.

Yes, the awakening of Kundalini might seem like a crazy experience that could lead you to situations beyond human control. Yet, that is only a part of the process. Kundalini is, in reality, an organic and intelligent process with a systematic purpose at the end.

An awakened Kundalini helps you untie all the emotional and mental knots in your mind so that you can see the true purpose of your life, in particular, and the universe, in general. The awakening of the Kundalini is the rising of Shakti within you. It also means the path for Shiva to enter you is getting cleared and ready.

Kundalini awakening means Shakti is calling out to Shiva to come down and meet Her even as She climbs up to meet Him. Kundalini Awakening is an exercise to bring divinity into our materialistic world more than trying to transcend our life. Kundalini Awakening is a process of purifying our body, mind, and soul so we become containers ready to receive and hold the universal divine power within us.

From a physiological perspective, you can relate the awakening of the Kundalini to the functioning of your central nervous system. When the Kundalini activates, the hitherto dormant energy moves up the Sushumna Nadi from chakra to chakra until it reaches the top of the head or the crown chakra. The central nervous system in our body functions in the same way. The primary aspects of the central nervous system are located in the spine, and it transmits signals between the rest of the body and the brain (or the top of the head).

Kundalini Awakening is frequently seen as a divine revelation as it comes with a multitude of mystical experiences like connectedness with the entire universe, bliss, beautiful colors and lights, and perception of beyond-human planes of consciousness. The truth, interestingly, is that Kundalini Awakening is nothing more than the first step of a long journey back to where you come from. When you wake up the dormant, sleeping Shakti, the real work is just about to begin.

If you have gone through the process of spiritual healing and purification, then it would be a smooth and not-so-difficult transition that happens when the Kundalini awakens. However, if the Shakti awakens before you are ready or if you are in a hurry, then the experience can be quite unpleasant.

Effectively, when the Kundalini awakens, it is like waking up a sleeping giant or giantess, in this case. She will purify your body, heart, and mind. However, if you have the Kundalini before you have dealt with the problems and other unpleasant aspects of your life, then the "cleansing" process can hit you really hard. Therefore, it is imperative that you don't force the awakening of the Kundalini. Let Her wake up in Her own time when She knows you are ready to accept Her in the active state.

The process of purification needed before the Kundalini Shakti is woken up can be difficult and intense. You might need to be hospitalized or even institutionalized, as it can be quite disorienting to live in the materialistic world with a fully awakened Kundalini. Once She wakes up, then your world will never be the same.

Therefore, if you are keen on awakening the Kundalini Shakti lying latent in you, then make sure you truly understand its potential impact. Understand how deep your desires are, and know that the path will not be easy. Finally, remind yourself that if you do awaken the Kundalini, you could face a situation where you wish you hadn't woken HER up.

Awakening the Kundalini Shakti is not just about psychic powers and bliss and oneness with the universe. It is also the hard work involved in the spiritual path. However, once SHE is awake, then SHE is in control, and you can only do what you have to do. So, take a decision after thoroughly thinking things through.

Symptoms of Kundalini Awakening

One of the first signs of Kundalini Awakening is certain inexplicable physical symptoms. If you have any such physical symptoms, visit a doctor and get yourself medically and physically examined and tested to rule out any medical issues. Regardless of the intensity and strangeness of physical symptoms you might experience, remember to be connected with reality at all times. Look after yourself, nourish your body well, exercise regularly, and ensure you have no cause for medical concern.

The initial outcomes of Kundalini Awakening can range from a simple deep yearning to know and connect with God to an intense feeling of something like a heatwave moving up your spine and bursting out at the crown chakra or the top of your head. Frequently, you will feel a sense of bliss or oneness with everything and everyone around you as your reality and consciousness expands to cover a lot more in this universe than what you sense current with your human body and senses.

You could feel total bliss accompanied by sudden body jerks that may freak you out. Just try to remain connected to yourself and your human reality during such episodes. Another interesting phenomenon of Kundalini Awakening is that whether you are a yoga practitioner or not, you will find yourself spontaneously moving into yoga postures and asanas you have never done before. Here are common experiences of going through the process of Kundalini Awakening:

- You spontaneously begin a journey of an emotional reckoning. You find yourself looking at your past life, either missing certain things or feeling sad that you had to experience unpleasant events.

- You will spend a lot of time and energy on unpacking and clearing emotional and mental clutter in your life. This is the best time to look at everything that makes you sad and let it go.

- You could have physical symptoms in the form of excessive sweating, waking up during the night without rhyme or reason, and sometimes even crying.

- You could get a sudden desire to make radical changes in your life. This need for change could cover any aspects of your life, including your friends, job, relationships, diet, exercise regimens, and more. Most important, you will realize what and why certain things are not working in your life.

- You become exceedingly conscious that your mind has been the only thing to have limited you from achieving your full potential. You realize that your ego has kept you trapped in a limited life despite knowing that the vast universe beckons you.

- You will certainly experience unbelievable synchronicities in your life. This means to say that certain things appear to fall into place automatically and aligned with your dreams and goals.

- Your ability to feel and sense others' emotions will improve significantly. This ability can be a huge put-off initially, considering that it will overwhelm you. However, this improvement in your empathic ability is the first sign of the opening of your third eye. You realize the power of seamless connectedness of everything in the universe.

- Also, you find it easy to see through people and know their real intentions usually masked behind forced behavior. Your ability to discern between good people and those who pretend to be increases significantly.

- You begin to look at everything around you with new eyes. Your view on religion, politics, tradition, etc. undergo a big change, and you wonder what you saw in them earlier.

- You feel a profound need to be of service to others, especially the ones who really need your help. You realize that helping people in need is the ultimate service one human can do for another.

When the Kundalini is awakened, an unprepared novice is likely to feel "out of sorts" or have what he or she believes to be "weird and unfamiliar experiences." They could feel disconnected from reality and can develop unique abilities, something that psychics and healers call the "sixth sense." Other symptoms of Kundalini awakening include:

- Increased and uncontrollable sensitivity to energy, sound, and light. Usually, the person feels all senses are on overload.
- A deep yearning for spiritual growth.
- Enhanced creativity.
- Intense compassion and love for others.
- An inexplicable feeling that something big in the spiritual realm is going to happen.
- Energetic sensations like internal lightning bolts running through your body.
- Uncontrollable jerky movements in the body of the practitioner.
- Feelings of having something creepy and crawly like snakes, ants, or spiders crawling all over your body, especially along the spine.
- Feeling intensely cold in all parts of the body except one of the chakra positions where you could feel intense heat.
- Spontaneous and automatic formation of asanas and kriyas (yoga postures), body-locking positions (Bandhas), mudras (hand gestures), and pranayama. Typically, the concerned person may never have learned or studied these hand and body movement techniques before.
- Waves of ecstatic bliss and pleasure, almost like an orgasm.
- Spontaneous breathing patterns as described in pranayama, even if the person experiencing it might never have heard about or learned it from anywhere.

- Sensations of strange sounds like a musical instrument or like a flute or violin playing, thunderclaps, sacred Sanskrit mantras, sounds of animals, drums beating, or anything else that others around the person cannot hear.

- Huge mood swings way beyond what the person is normally capable of.

- Waves of wisdom about the reality of life and the universe.

- Everything in the field of vision appears to vibrate and scintillatingly illuminated, leading to an understanding that everything is interconnected.

- Gastrointestinal disorders like nausea, vomiting, diarrhea, etc.

- Decreased or increased metabolic activity.

- Cramps, numbness, pain, and restlessness in the limbs.

Physical symptoms manifested in your body during Kundalini Awakening will be atypical and difficult to diagnose and/or treat using traditional drugs and medicines. The diagnosis will most often be explained as psychosomatic or an underlying emotional or mental problem that is unresolved.

Most of us have energy blockages and imbalances - along with energy-sapping lifestyle habits - which prevent us from drawing the full powers of our vitality to lead a fulfilling, meaningful life. Thanks to these energy blockages and imbalances, we feel our focus is scattered unproductively all over the place; we feel inexplicably fatigued and dull. Awakening the Kundalini helps people get rid of these blockages in multiple ways, including making their bodies move spontaneously into yogic postures.

These spontaneous yoga postures that your body gets into help to cleanse your system of all negative energies. The awakened Kundalini does this to help release accumulated emotional, physical, and mental knots in your body. The Kundalini drives you to move your body in ways that make it seem like you are performing yoga asanas. As the Kundalini awakens, all the past emotions you have kept under wraps –

or even forgotten about – leave your system. Feelings of denial, rejections, trauma, and everything else gets eliminated from your body and mind.

This process is difficult because the elimination of negativity does not happen smoothly if you are not prepared. With an awakened Kundalini, the universe will conspire to hasten the workings of your karma at a faster rate than before for which you might not be prepared. Therefore, forcing your Kundalini to awaken might be counterproductive to the ultimate spiritual goal of the exercise.

The trick with the process and outcomes of Kundalini Awakening is that if done in an unbalanced way, the practitioner could end up with something known in the spiritual world as Kundalini Syndrome. Kundalini Syndrome can be loosely defined as a collection of affective, sensory, mental, and motor experiences that are strange, unfamiliar, and fear-inducing.

With the awakening of the Kundalini, getting scared of exploring an unknown and strange realm is natural. It's important to remind you that Kundalini does not offer any magical cures for all your ills. What it offers you is the power to transcend the materialistic world spiritually and physically so you know and understand there is far much more in this universe than your life. This revelation will help you ground yourself and learn to accept and embrace all your life experiences with equanimity, even as you feel more empowered than before to handle the problems and issues in your routine life.

Some people who are thrust into this new experience find it difficult to cope with it. Therefore, they feel the need to seek refuge in alcohol, drugs, and other addictive substances. The best thing to help yourself deal with this fear is to educate yourself about Kundalini and its powers when awakened so you can prepare yourself well.

Awakening the Kundalini can have other unpleasant outcomes, including the end of certain relationships in your life, a reorientation of your professional and personal life, and undoing the habits of your old life. It can be painful because you might not want to give up certain people and things. Your attempts to hold on to them - even as you try to continue your journey of Kundalini awakening - can cause a lot of suffering both for you and the people in your life you are not ready to let go of.

It is vital to remember here that Kundalini is not an illness as the symptoms of "Kundalini Syndrome" described above might make novices believe it to be. When conditions are not right at the time of Kundalini Awakening, then the process can lead to psychological and physical maladies that appear as "disease-like" symptoms. Therefore, it is better to call these experiences as "signs of Kundalini Awakening" rather than symptoms.

The more work you do on yourself before the awakening of Kundalini, the smoother and easier the entire process will be. Spontaneous or forced-upon awakenings are not good because you will have a difficult road to pass through. It takes time and effort. But eventually, Kundalini Awakening transforms the practitioner's life at physical, emotional, and spiritual levels.

The benefits of an awakened Kundalini are numerous. You will become an empath because of your increased sensitivity to many energies around you. As an empath, you can make a positive impact on the people in your life. The psychic abilities because of Kundalini Awakening help in building your creative pursuits and personal charisma, naturally and with no side-effects. You will know and experience real peace, and nothing from the outside world will dent this sense of calmness you will achieve within you. The confounding mysteries of life will no longer remain a mystery to you.

Chapter 3: Kundalini and Meditation

Now that we are past the theoretical aspects of Kundalini Yoga, it is time to move ahead with practical work. So, how does one start Kundalini Yoga? Well, as mentioned earlier, the awakening process should happen slowly without rushing or forcing anything on yourself. This chapter is focused on getting you started on simple meditation techniques that will help you increase self-awareness and concentration powers.

These basic meditation techniques are critical to learn and master because through them you will not only identify your strengths and weaknesses but also come to terms with multiple past and present unpleasant aspects of your personality. The more you learn about yourself, the better control you will have on your life.

Accepting positive personality traits and other positive aspects of our life is usually easy for most of us. However, acknowledging our weaknesses, embracing them, and loving ourselves despite them is a skill that requires some practice. Basic meditation techniques that focus on non-judgmental observations of our life experiences are a great way to get started on this journey of self-discovery. So, let's get started.

Most of us live our lives mindlessly running from one task to another without even being aware of what we are doing, and sometimes, even why we are doing it. We wake up each morning, rush through our morning ablutions, gobble up our breakfast, rush through heavy traffic to reach our workplace, and work from morning to night until it is time to go home and fall asleep completely enervated and exhausted.

Often, most of us feel like we don't have a purpose in life. We don't even know what our desires and intentions are. We do most things in life because other people do or because it's a fad. We want to make money because others see it as a way to succeed. We want to become famous because that seems to be the thing to do today. We really don't know ourselves or what we truly want in life.

The first step toward decluttering yourself from this rush of life is to start meditating. Meditation helps you live life with increased awareness and heightened intention. Kundalini meditation is an advanced form of meditation where you try to awaken your Kundalini. But before that, let us start with some basics.

What is Meditation?

Meditation is a structured process using various techniques such as mindfulness through which the practitioner learns to focus his or her mind on an object, activity, or thought to build increased self-awareness and focused attention. Meditation helps the practitioner achieve a calm, clear, and uncluttered state of mind.

Meditation has been practiced by humans for eons. It has been an important tenet of multiple religions where followers have used it to pursue spiritual enlightenment and self-realization. The earliest known records of meditation are found in Hindu texts like the Vedas and the Upanishads, where the idea is called "Dhyana." Meditation is also found in Buddhism, especially in the form of mindfulness.

Since the beginning of the 19th century, the concept and practice of meditation and mindfulness have spread to the western world. Scientific research continues to be done on this fascinating subject. Thanks to the positive outcomes of these research studies, meditation practice is part of multiple therapies used by western medical doctors and physicians.

Meditation has become an important tool in the field of psychiatry and psychology, and research on using it as a complementary therapy to treat numerous psychological and mental diseases is ongoing, many of which hold much promise. All this goes to show that the human mind plays an important role in our lives, including the way our personality turns out, the way we behave, and the way we live. However, most of us underplay, knowingly or unknowingly, the importance of training our minds to lead better lives. Meditation is a great way to train your mind consciously so you can use its deep powers to bring about positive changes in your life.

So, let us start by finding answers to some of the basic questions on meditation, including:

- Where and when to meditate?
- What should I do with my body while I meditate?
- How long should I meditate?
- What should I do with my mind while I meditate?
- How often should I meditate?

Where and when should you meditate? Technically, you can meditate anywhere and at any time. You can sit on a chair, on the floor, or even while lying in bed. Why? Because meditating is an exercise for the mind and not the body. However, there is an optimal way to meditate so you get maximum benefits. For example, meditating while lying on the bed may not be such a great idea because you could fall asleep unintentionally.

Sitting on the floor with your back erect but relaxed is considered the best way to meditate. This position allows you to remain wide awake, and sitting in this position can actually be comfortable for long periods even if initially, you are not used to it. With practice, you will see that sitting on the floor is one of the best ways to meditate. And yet, if you have a problem sitting cross-legged on the floor, you can sit on a chair with your back erect.

Also, choose a location free from distractions and disturbances. Make sure it is a comfortable place not very hot or cold. A bottle of water next to you might help if you want to take a short break . Choose your clothes wisely too so you don't feel uncomfortable, considering kinds of fabric can stick to your skin and cause you to itch or scratch, which could distract you from your meditation. Light-colored, fresh, clean clothes make you feel fresh and light and are conducive to meditation.

What should you do with your body while you meditate? The feet are the most important body parts of the body to focus on while meditating. Sitting on the floor with one foot over the other is recommended to be the best by experienced meditators and followers.

However, if this position is not possible (especially in the early stages of learning and practicing meditation), then it is perfectly all right to sit cross-legged with one leg over the other. Your arms should be resting on your thighs, and your palms should rest on top of each other, forming the shape of a cup and resting on your folded legs.

Your back should be erect but not stiff. A relaxed position with no discomfort in any part of your body is critical to meditation. Your head should be straight, neither tilted upwards or downwards. Your eyes can be open or closed while you meditate. However, in the initial days of practice, if you keep your eyes open, you are likely to get distracted with the surrounding sights, making it difficult to focus. Therefore, as a beginner, it is better to meditate with your eyes closed to enhance the ease of achieving focus. If, however, you do meditate with your eyes open, it is best not to focus on any object or thing in front of you. It is better to look into the distance.

The time of meditation is up to you. The trick is to find a time when you know you will not be disturbed by anything or anyone. Also, don't meditate when feeling excessively hungry or overly full, as the unpleasantness in your stomach might distract you from your meditation.

Considering these elements, it might be best to meditate as soon as you wake up before others in your home wake up and distract you. Do it just before going to bed after others have fallen asleep. Remember that you can meditate at any time of the day or night when you feel like it.

How long should you meditate? In the initial days, it might be a good idea not to set the timer for very long. This is because time tends to go slower than normal when meditating. When time passes slowly, and you are not yet used to sitting quietly for long, then your mind is likely to be disturbed and distracted by thoughts of how much longer it will be before the end of the session.

So, start with a short period, maybe five minutes (or even less if you want). Learn to sit still quietly for the chosen period until you are comfortable. Then you can gradually increase this duration until you can meditate for at least 30 minutes at a stretch.

What to do with your mind during meditation? Here is the actual trick in meditation. There are a variety of elements and things that meditators use to focus their minds on during the meditation session. For example, in some meditation, you would need to focus on an object ahead of you. Some meditation techniques involve chanting mantras.

One of the most basic forms of meditation that is best suited for beginners is mindfulness breathing meditation. It is not only easy to learn (mastering it will take time and diligent practice), but it is as powerful as any other form of meditation, including reciting complex mantras. As the name suggests, the focus of this meditation type is your breath.

First, make sure you are breathing through your nose and not through your mouth. Once you get this right, you need only to focus on your breath and observe the way the air enters and leaves your nostrils as you breathe in and breathe out. Observe the way the air feels as it flows into and out of your nostrils as you inhale and exhale.

Watch how your breath transitions from inhalation to exhalation. Observe that small (almost indiscernible) pause between the inhalation and exhalation. Observe everything about your breathing process. Do not try to control your breath, either slowing it down or hastening it. Just observe in a non-judgment way, without criticizing, praising, or forming any opinions in your mind.

What you will notice soon enough is that thoughts will come into your mind sooner rather than later, distracting you from this task of observing your breath. So, simple as it might seem, this exercise calls for your full attention to the task at hand. Your thoughts are so numerous and varied that you will notice how each thought moves into the next uncontrollably. For example, you could have these thoughts:

- I wonder what I should cook for dinner. Maybe take-out?
- What my friend did today was wrong. I feel so hurt. I wish I could have said something to her.
- I hope my daughter finished her homework today
- I have to take my mother to the hospital tomorrow.
- I hope I finish my project on time.

Don't force your way into or out of any thought that comes to distract you. Stay with the thought until it goes away, and then gently get your attention back on your breath. It will take time to master this technique because your thoughts will continuously come and distract you. Allow them to distract you. Controlling your thoughts would be counterproductive. As each thought passes and before your mind moves to the next one, try to bring your attention back to your breath. Repeat this exercise for the entire duration of the meditation session.

When you try to do this for the first time, getting yourself to focus only on your breath for even a couple of seconds will be a huge challenge. You will find yourself lost in your thoughts often. Sometimes, you may even realize that you never focused on your breath during the entire meditation session. That doesn't matter. Just remind yourself to try again and repeat the meditation session the next day. One small tip that might come in handy for you is to focus your attention on that small, almost indiscernible gap between inhalation and exhalation.

Other common distractions would be in itches, irritations, frustrations (especially wondering when it will end), etc. Don't worry if you find it difficult to overcome them. Don't feel guilty or critical of yourself. It is normal in the initial days. Each time you are distracted, try to bring back the focus of your mind on your breath.

Mindfulness breathing technique is simple to understand and learn but difficult to master. Mastering takes a lot of time and effort. The important thing to know that when you focus on your breath even for a short while, the sense of peace and calm is amazing. Also, you get better with dedicated practice and repeated trial and error. You will notice that the more you practice, the longer you can focus on your breath at each of your sessions. Remember not to be frustrated or impatient with yourself. Don't give yourself deadlines of any kind. Just keep doing it daily, and you will get there.

How often should you meditate? This question has been answered, right? Every day! Remind yourself that your mind is like a muscle. The more you make it work, the stronger it will get. Meditate every single day, even if it is just for five minutes. Don't try to increase the duration until you are sure you want to. The trick lies in meditating every single day!

You can choose to do twice a day for five minutes each or once for 10 minutes. Choose a convenient time, place, and duration. The important thing is to meditate every day without fail so you can harness all the benefits of meditation and get ready to move into the next step of Kundalini Yoga.

When can you experience the benefits of meditation? Well, this question has no one-solution-for-all answer because it differs from person to person and also on the frequency and intensity of the meditation practice. Some people are naturally attuned to mindfulness and can catch on to the practice faster and quicker than others with a problem being mindful and staying focused.

However, it takes about a month of diligent meditation practice for 20 minutes each day before you can even think of reaping the multiple benefits of meditation. You will see your ability to manage negative emotions improving considerably. You will be in a calmer and happier frame of mind than before, regardless of external circumstances. You will notice you have a reduced tendency to be judgmental about anything or anyone. You find it easier to see all perspectives with an open mind facilitating your ability to make informed and non-impulsive choices.

Benefits of Meditation

Just to collectively show you the various benefits of meditation, here is a small (and definitely not exhaustive) list:

- Improves concentration and helps to keep out random thoughts from throwing you off balance.
- Breaks off the auto-pilot way of life and brings in increased awareness and mindfulness into your routine.
- Helps to balance your body, mind, and soul.
- Helps in improving and building creative energy to handle problems and issues in your life easily.
- Improves awareness of your body and its various problems and weaknesses, including the issues in your lifestyle.

- Improves nerve connections, patterns in the brain, and keeps you emotionally and mentally balanced. It also improves cognitive functioning.

- Helps reduce stress and anxiety and also enhances peace of mind.

- Helps reduce sleep disorders and improves sleeping patterns.

- Proper breathing techniques during meditation help to improve lung capacity.

Meditation is a simple exercise. The trick is to make it into a daily habit so you can benefit from it. Once you have learned how to meditate and have been able to harness its benefits in your life, you are one step closer to Kundalini Awakening.

Chapter 4: Working with Chakras

The concept of chakras has been introduced to you briefly in this book. The Kundalini Shakti, when awakened, moves up your spine, passes through the various chakras until it reaches the top of your head or the Crown chakra. Let us understand more about Chakras in this chapter.

Understanding Chakras

In Sanskrit, Chakra translates to "wheel" or "disk." Therefore, chakras can be visualized as spinning disks or wheels of light and/or energy. The chakras in our body absorb and maintain energy levels in our body and mind for its smooth, optimal, and unhindered function.

Chakras, or the energy centers in our subtle body, represent the energetic connection between our consciousness and our physical body. They are seven important chakras, and each is in a constant flux of energy, receiving and transmitting it, involuntarily and without our knowledge, until we try to become conscious of their power.

The smooth functioning of our chakras determines multiple aspects of your life, including:

- The depth with which you experience your life.

- How deeply and mindfully engaged you are with every moment of your life.

- How much inner peace you experience.

- How successful you are in your personal and professional relationships.

- And even how to fit your physical body is.

Working with your chakras, realigning imbalanced chakras, and ensuring their smooth function will help in the uninterrupted flow of subtle and spiritual energy in your body. This smooth energy flow facilitates a happier and more meaningful life than before, even as you prepare yourself to awaken your Kundalini Shakti.

By practicing regular activation of the seven important chakras in your body, you can tap into their vast reservoir of spiritual energy that can easily overflow to positively affect all other aspects of your life. Each root chakra has a bija mantra (seed sound or its basic sound) along with its set of functions and responsibilities. Let us look at each of these seven prominent chakras or energy centers in our body in detail.

Root Chakra

The Sanskrit word for this energy center is Muladhara, its bija mantra is *I am*, and it says, "I exist." The root chakra, as the name suggests, helps you root your body and mind to the power of the earth. It is related to the basic survival energy that we all need to live well in this world. When you were in your mother's womb, the root chakra was the only thing that mattered. The root chakra provided you with your survival kit, including nourishment, warmth, stability, and security, which are survival-related elements.

The root chakra is the seat of your instincts, the true power behind your survival. The primal fight/flight response is only a manifestation of your Muladhara. A strong, grounded Muladhara empowers you to lead a materialistically happy life, free from physical suffering. The root chakra grounds you and empowers you to deal with the trials and tribulations of life.

Location of the root chakra - The root chakra is at the base of your spine between your anus and genitals. The color associated with the root chakra is red.

Here are important aspects of the Muladhara:

- It helps in building a strong, grounded connection to your body.

- It facilitates your ability to have insights into relationships.

- It frees you from biases and prejudices and empowers you to make informed, objective choices in all matters in your life.

- It frees you from inherited negative perspectives.

- It empowers you to value all life on earth.

- It grounds you and builds security and stability in your life.

- It builds your commitment levels.

Imbalances in the energy of the root chakra can cause anxiety and stress. You could be inexplicably scared of everything around you. Physical manifestations of an unbalanced root chakra include problems in the colon, bladder, lower back, feet and legs, prostate (for men), and eating disorders.

Balancing your root chakra - Use these exercises to help you balance and harmonize the energy in your root chakra. The basic tenet of these exercises is to stand on your feet mindfully and connected with the earth element. The best part is you can do these exercises anywhere, whether while you are waiting in line at a grocery store, or teller counter, or waiting for your train or bus.

- Stand comfortably with your feet apart (the width of your hip) and firmly fixed on the ground. Your heels should be aligned with your hips while in your standing position. Shift the weight of your body from one foot to another slowly until you are satisfied that each is getting an equal amount of your body weight.

- Observe your stance carefully and check if you stand on your foot or on your heels. Gently rock yourself back and forth until your center of gravity is felt at the midpoint of the arches of your feet.

- Make sure all parts of your feet are getting equal amounts of your body weight on them.

- Feel the balls of all the ten toes and make sure they are firmly gripping the ground.

- Feel the bones of your shin pushing down. Ensure your knees are straight but not stiff or locked. Feel the bones in your thighs, calves, and tailbone as they carry the weight of your body. Push your lower ribs inwards.

- Keep your shoulder straight and your head erect, ensuring your chin is parallel to the ground.

- Focus on your breath and ensure you are breathing normally and rhythmically. Experience the feeling of being free and stable when your feet are firmly placed on the ground, and your body knows that it is secure.

With this strong, stable, free, and powerful physical posture, look at the other aspects of your life and find answers to the question, "Where do I stand?"

Also, physical exercises like jumping, jogging, dancing, etc. are also very useful to clear the energy blocks and balance the root chakra. Other ways of enhancing the power and energy of the root chakra are:

Sacral Chakra

The Sanskrit term for this energy center is Swadisthana. Its bija mantra is *vam*, and it says, "I desire." Associated with the pleasure impulse, creative instincts, and being the seat of the instinct of procreation, a balanced and free-flowing sacral chakra brings grace, allure, and fluidity in your life. Your ability to accept and adapt to changes increases automatically.

Unlike the root chakra, the sacral chakra is not associated with survival. It is more skewed toward the gratification of your senses and pleasure seeking. The power of the sacral chakra lies in fulfilling its desires. Symbolized by the water element, unblocked energy flow in the Swadisthana empowers you with the strength of movement and adaptability. It enables you to give and take to and from others with gratitude and humility.

The more balanced your sacral chakra is, the more comfortable you are with yourself. While you will be happy to share your energy and love with others, you will also know the importance of fulfilling your own needs. The sacral chakra is also responsible for sexuality, intimacy, passion, money, joy, and creativity.

Location of the sacral chakra - It is located just above the pubic bone, and orange is the color associated with it.

Importance of a balanced sacral chakra - A balanced sacral chakra helps to increase your creativity, vitality, and sensitivity. You will feel empowered to express your emotions in healthy and confident ways, thereby enhancing your ability to have fulfilling relationships and partnerships. The sacral chakra is considered feminine and is an important element to have an open and honest personality allowing yourself to nurture yourself and those around you.

An unbalanced or blocked sacral chakra can make you unemotional and insecure. You are likely to feel uncertainty, making you weak-minded, and leading to a decreased ability to cope with and adapt to changes in your life. A sense of detachment and a rigid outlook on everything will make it difficult to ride through the ups and downs of your life. Here are mental exercises that will help in balancing and unblocking your Swadisthana. It is a visualization process where you imagine your mind to be a vast, open lake.

• Sit comfortably in a meditating position. Breathe normally through your nostrils. Ensure your mouth is closed.

- Now, imagine your mind to be a vast, open lake. Next, visualize someone dropping a large, blue diamond into the lake, creating ripples in the lake.

- Allow your breathing to progressively become shallow until the air appears to be coming to the end of your nostrils. This approach will ensure your breath creates no ripples on the lake of your mind.

- As your breath becomes calmer, your mind will also become calmer, and the ripples on the lake will slowly but surely fade away.

- Now, focus your attention on looking for the diamond through the depths of the clear water.

- Your thoughts will scatter, especially initially. Each time you notice this happening, bring your attention back to locating the diamond beneath the lake water.

- Importantly, don't struggle with control, or suppress your thoughts because the more you try to avoid or suppress your thoughts, the stronger they will return.

- These suppressed thoughts will sap your energy needlessly. Instead, observe them with indifference, and the chances of them moving on without disturbing your peace are high.

- Attempt to focus only on locating the diamond. As the lake water becomes calmer and ripples slowly reduce, you can see right to its bottom. As you scan through the floor of the lake, you will find the shining piece of blue diamond.

The same thing holds good for your mind. Keep it calm and free from anxiety, and you can dive into its depths and find your diamond, the power of your inner peace.

Solar Plexus Chakra

Known as the Manipura in Sanskrit, the solar plexus chakra provides you with the transformational power to process matter and energy. Its bija mantra is the *ram*, and it says, "I control." The power in this energy center helps you convert everything you take in, including food, ideas, observations, etc., into practical and usable forms. Your sense of self and self-worth, the most prized possession for any person, is held in Manipura. It is also the seat of your personality and charisma. When the energy flows freely in the solar plexus chakra, the world can perceive your authentic personality.

The element connected with this chakra is fire, and just like how fire (also manifested as the sun's energy) gives life to earth, the heat of your solar plexus enlivens your body and mind. Fire is an important element in multiple traditions and cultures. In Hindu tradition, marriages are performed with the fire as the witness when vows are exchanged between the couple. In any fire ceremony, offerings and prayers are sent up to the gods through the fire in the main altar. Therefore, this vital element is seen as a messenger and as an interface between the human world and the higher realms of consciousness, most of which are not accessible to the average human.

Your digestive system (which converts consumed food into usable energy molecules) is controlled by the solar plexus chakra. As the name suggests, this chakra is in the solar plexus region, in the stomach area, just above the belly button. Yellow is the color associated with the sacral chakra.

Importance of a balanced solar plexus chakra - The solar plexus chakra is responsible for the following elements in your life:

- It empowers your willpower and assertiveness.
- It helps you establish healthy boundaries in your life.
- It is an essential energy center to help you connect with your own inner power.
- It helps in the smooth functioning of the digestive system and metabolism.
- It not only boosts your stamina levels but also helps you know when you have breached your limits so you can quit in time.

The symptoms of a blocked or unbalanced solar plexus chakra include:

- Lack of self-trust.
- Low self-esteem.
- Compromised willpower.
- The mentality of being a victim in all situations.
- Poor digestion resulting in various metabolic-related problems including nausea, diarrhea, low physical energy, and more.
- Inability to take responsibility.
- Being unreliable.

Use the following exercise to get back the power of your solar plexus chakra:

When the digestive fire seated in the solar plexus region burns brightly and healthily, then your body can optimally absorb the nutrients from the consumed food and the vital energy from the air you breathe. In such circumstances, you have an intelligent and deep connection with the world around you. In a contrasting situation, both your body and mind will become weak, resulting in chronic physiological and psychological imbalances.

Fasting on juices and liquids once a week is a great way to regain the balance of your solar plexus chakra. Juice fasting gives your digestive system a much-needed break from its relentless working condition. Consequently, your body and mind can cleanse themselves and clear energy blockages in the solar plexus chakra.

Another important and useful outcome of juice fasting is that when your belly is not overly full, your ego's defense mechanism decreases, which, in turn, opens your heart to accept and absorb the positivity around you. You develop a healthy personality with improved self-confidence, mental resolve and willpower. Here is a small juice diet you can follow to rebalance your solar plexus chakra:

- Drink 2-3 liters of fruit and vegetable juices right through the day. Just to give you a rough estimate, 2-3 liters would be about 3.5 to 5.5 pints.

- Make your juices at home and ensure you don't use over three types of fruit and vegetables. Also, do not combine fruit and vegetables to make the juices. Have vegetable juice or fruit juice separately and not in the same glass of juice.

- Cabbage, carrots, and fresh ginger roots are excellent choices considering their special benefits in cleansing and balancing your Manipura. Try to avoid fleshy fruits such as bananas, avocados, pineapples, etc.

- During the day of the fast, eat no solid foods, fizzy drinks or caffeine. Avoid tea and coffee, although herbal teas like mint tea, chamomile tea, green tea, etc. are great options. Ensure you drink plenty of water to flush out all the accumulated toxins from your body.

- If you have a headache, drink a glass of hot water with a squeeze of lime juice.

The fasting day should be a quiet, meditative time. Spend the day meditating as often as you can. Try to connect with all your thoughts. Practice yoga and include simple breathing exercises as well. Choose a day wisely when you know you can indulge on a fasting day without being excessively disturbed by personal or professional problems.

Heart Chakra

Known as *Anahata* in Sanskrit, the heart chakra is the energetic core of your subtle body. The bija mantra of the heart chakra is *yam*, and it says, "I love." Located in the heart region, the color green is associated with the heart chakra. This energy center is one of the most powerful portals in your body that connects the spiritual and the physical realms. The primary function of the heart chakra is to transform the subtle energies of the three chakras above it into usable, practical forms that can be visible and manifested in the physical realm. The heart chakra facilitates the downward movement of energy and helps in transforming consciousness into tangible, physical matter.

Also, the heart chakra does the reverse process, so it transforms physical energies and matter from the lower three chakras into subtler ideas and thoughts. The combination of these two contrasting functions of the heart chakra makes it one of the most complex energy centers to understand and balance.

Your heart chakra empowers expression of selfless love and compassion and drives you to give your best both to yourself and to others. A healthy heart chakra makes it possible for you to embrace everything happening in your life and whatever your life offers. When your heart chakra is awakened and balanced, you feel that life touches you at every moment.

The heart chakra is like the CPU for the other chakras and controls many of the minor chakras all over the body. Here is a classic illustration of a person's behavior and outcome when his or her Anahata is perfectly balanced and free. Suppose this person's friend is grieving the loss of a loved one. If this heart chakra-empowered person simply places his or her hand over the mourner's shoulders, he or she feels immediate relief, as if a huge burden has been lifted, and that everything will be all right.

Importance of a balanced heart chakra - When the energy flow in your heart chakra is unhindered and well-balanced, then:

- You find yourself emotionally balanced.
- Your ability to perform heart-centered work and tasks improves considerably.
- You learn to forgive people who have harmed you.
- You learn to let go of negativity.

If there is a blockage in your Anahata, then you could experience:

- Excessive shyness.
- Depression, anxiety, and loneliness.

- Difficulty in forgiving and letting go.

- Difficulty in feeling empathy for others.

People with a blocked heart chakra are usually regarded as hard-hearted. Loneliness will plague you if you don't clear and balance your Anahata. Use these recommendations and exercises to the right of the imbalance and blockages in your heart chakra.

The lotus hand mudra (or hand gesture that resembles a lotus) is a very useful tool to cleanse and balance your heart chakra. You can practice it any time, especially when you feel emotionally enervated, misunderstood, or exploited. It helps you overcome the pain of loneliness and despair too.

The lotus mudra helps you open yourself to accept divine and universal help and gets you ready to receive what you need during your difficult time. Regular practice of this hand gesture will help you find unconditional love and genuine affection.

The hand gesture representing the blossoming of a lotus flower represents your heart opening up. Like the lotus with a deep resolve to climb upwards and away from the mire in which it grows, your heart chakra will be empowered to break through the shackles of lower energies and move upwards towards universal power. In Hinduism, the lotus flower represents our inner beauty with the power to emerge from darkness and troubles. Use these steps to form the lotus mudra:

- Bring your palms together at your chest. Keep your fingers pointed upwards and relaxed.

- Keep the base and the fingertips of both your hands touching each other. Bend your fingers slightly outward so the hand gesture looks like a lotus bud.

- Next, keep the base and the edges of the thumbs and little fingers together. Open out the other fingers, making the gesture look like a blooming flower. This opening gesture represents the opening of your heart.

- Breathe deeply about 4-5 times repeating the affirmation, "I am ready to receive whatever life offers me."

- When satisfied with your affirmation, bring your fingers together again, and form the shape of a lotus bud.

- Repeat this mudra as often as you can or want.

Throat Chakra

Known as *Vishuddha* in Sanskrit, the energy in the throat chakra is the seat of communication of your subtle body. Its bija mantra is *ham*, and it says, "I express." The throat chakra (at the throat; its color is light blue) is responsible for your speaking and listening skills. When this chakra is out of balance, or there is a blockage, there is a communication impediment between your mind and heart.

Your mind cannot process the emotions arising from your heart. Your ability to process the emotions correctly and sensibly would be compromised, resulting in impulsive and irrational behaviors. An open and balanced throat chakra will help your ideas and thoughts be concretized according to your needs.

The throat chakra is the seat of language, and not of emotions, which sits in the heart chakra. Even as it can express positive words and blessing articulately, the throat chakra can also spit out venomous and hurting words, if not balanced or if the energy is blocked. The biggest and most obvious thing you will notice if your throat chakra is blocked is your increased difficulty in communicating effectively.

So, when the energy is free flowing in the throat chakra, your words will be kind, compassionate, thoughtful, and truthful. Your voice will be vibrant and strong. Your writing, reading, speaking, and articulation skills will be at their best levels. Also, you can listen well when others are speaking. You are as comfortable with silence as you are with talking and using words.

Physical symptoms of a blocked throat chakra include a hoarse or raspy voice, mouth ulcers, chronic sore throat, laryngitis, gum and teeth related diseases, thyroid problems, swollen glands, tonsillitis, and even cancer in the throat region.

Importance of the throat chakra - The Vishuddha is responsible for:

- Improved communication, articulation and creativity.

- Public-speaking and oratory skills.

- Art forms like singing and dancing.

- Making your face, voice and body more expressive and articulate.

- Developing your inner voice.

Freeing up blocked energies and imbalances in your throat chakra calls for improving and strengthening your physical communication skills through singing, dancing, public speaking, story-telling, and more. You can strengthen the power of your inner voice by investing time and energy in daily journaling. Even painting is a great way to build energy in your throat chakra. Here are some self-questions you should try to find answers to. Your quest to find answers to these questions will help a lot in clearing the blockages in your throat chakra.

- Do I live authentically?

- What aspects of my life do I find it difficult to face and accept the truth?

- Are my words, actions, and thoughts in synchronicity with each other?

- Do I dominate conversations?

- Do I find it difficult to open up and speak in front of others because I fear making a scene or embarrassing myself?

- How frequently do I break my promises? Please include even the small promises like being on time for dates, meetings, etc.

- Do the words I use hurt or empower the people around me?

- Are my intentions hidden or easily visible to others?

- Do I express my ideas and thoughts as the "only truth?"

- What are the unfinished conversations in my life that haunt me and prevent me from opening up and speaking confidently?

Brow or Third Eye Chakra

Called as *Ajna* Chakra in Sanskrit, the energy center on your brow or forehead is also called the "third eye." The bija mantra of the third eye chakra is *Om* or *Aum*, and it says, "I am the witness." Located between the eyes in the forehead area, the color of the third eye chakra is indigo. This energy center is the command center of your subtle body. It is the seat of judgment, the root of intellectualism, rationality, wisdom and emotional intelligence. The power of the Ajna Chakra helps you develop abstract thinking, symbolic and theoretical concepts, and build organizational skills.

The brow chakra is also the seat of your "sixth sense," which is believed to manage and control the basic five senses of humans. It also regulates the five lower chakras and the nadis (energy channels) leading from and into them. Six important spiritual powers are connected with the Ajna Chakra including:

1. Thought control

2. Directing your attention and focus

3. Perfect concentration

4. Undisturbed and unobstructed meditation

5. Enlightenment

6. The state of Samadhi or the state of super-consciousness

Importance of the third eye or brow chakra - The third eye chakra and the energy held in it are responsible for the following:

- Developing your innate instinctive and intuitive powers.

- Cultivating imagination and creativity.
- Your ability to have flexible thought processes and viewpoints.
- Your power to cross the mundane planes of consciousness and wander into the higher planes.
- At a physical level, the third eye chakra governs our brains.
- Its energy is connected to the working of our minds, at a subtler level.

An unbalanced and blocked Ajna Chakra could manifest physically in the form of:

- Frequent headaches.
- Poor eyesight.
- Learning disability.
- Frequent nightmares and/or insomnia.
- Forgetfulness.
- Epileptic seizures.
- Alzheimer's and other cognitive and mental disorders.
- Even brain hemorrhages, tumors, or a stroke, in extreme cases.

Mental and emotional symptoms of an unbalanced or blocked Ajna Chakra include:

- You jump to conclusions and could be indecisive about various matters in your life.
- You could be in a constant state of mental confusion.
- A misplaced sense of self-righteousness.
- A vain outlook, especially about your intellectual abilities.
- You could live in an illusionary world, have hallucinations, and can be totally disconnected from reality.

Use the Bhuchari meditation technique and process to balance your third eye chakra. This meditation requires you to gaze into void space. Follow these steps.

- Sit comfortably in your preferred meditative posture, facing a white wall. As usual, make sure your spine and shoulders are erect, but overall that your body is relaxed.

- Bring your right hand toward your face. Touch the tip of your thumb to your upper lip. Fold the fore, middle, and ring fingers downward and gently point your little finger outward. This gesture would be similar to the "drinking water" gesture you would use if you couldn't talk.

- Now, stare gently at the tip of your little finger with a steady gaze. Try not to blink while you stare. Avoid trying to force a steady, unblinking gaze because then you could get tense. Just gaze steadily and gently at the tip of your little finger.

- After a while, tears might start rolling down your eyes. This is good for cleansing your eyes, sinuses and tear ducts. Practice this exercise for 5 minutes every day. Then, drop the use of your hands, and try to gaze at the place where your finger was. Start this gazing into the void exercise for 5 minutes each day, and slowly take it to about 15 minutes.

This exercise is not just good for your eyes and sinuses, but also a powerful energy cleanser for your Ajna Chakra. It promotes your ability for intense concentration and focus.

Crown Chakra

The Crown Chakra or the Sahasrara in Sanskrit, is the gateway to the place of infinite consciousness. At the top of your head, the color purple is associated with the crown chakra. There are many bija mantras for the crown, including Om, Soham, and Aah. It says, "I am that I am."

This chakra is the portal in your subtle body through which you can connect with and experience what the yogis and sages of India call "Satchidananda" or eternal bliss from Absolute Knowledge. Breaching the crown chakra takes you beyond the realm of your individual awareness (or Chitta, in Sanskrit).

Therefore, the Sahasrara empowers you to transcend the mundane life of duality, which refers to the idea that everything we see and experience is separate from us and from each other. When the crown chakra is fully energized, you get to experience the interconnectedness with all things in the universal.

The Sahasrara is at the top of the Sushumna Nadi (or the central channel through which the energy flows in your body). The other two primary nadis, namely Pingala and Ida (both of which are limited to the ordinary consciousness), cannot reach the top of the Sushumna Nadi.

Importance of the crown chakra - Empowering and energizing your crown chakra builds your intuitive knowledge, and enhances your sense of wonder as you see and experience everything within and around you in the light of universal connectedness. It will also help you form strong spiritual connections, and you will have a deeper understanding of the universal, the world, and yourself than before. You will be empowered to discover and experience "divine" mysteries that go beyond the human world. Breaching the Sahasrara empowers you with a sense of being complete in all respects.

People who work successfully with the energy of their crown chakra are often seen as miracle workers - and it is easy to understand why. These people are divinely guided by what they see when they cross the threshold of human intelligence, a place that ordinary mortals cannot reach regularly. So, the crown chakra is the seat of:

- Deeper understanding
- Intuitive knowledge and power
- Powerful spiritual connections

- Experience and discovery of divine mysteries

- Increased sense of wonder

- Experience of completeness

- Connection to the universal divine power

Imbalances and blockages in your crown chakra are likely to be manifested in these ways:

- You will notice that your heart, body and mind are all working on each of their own paths, and they are not aligned with each other.

- You will find yourself being excessively self-centered as you cannot see or experience the interconnectedness of life and the universe.

- Your energy aura will be limited to the lower chakra, resulting in a life of pure materialism and sensual pursuits.

- You lack in spiritual connection and awareness.

You limit your knowledge and beliefs to what your five senses can experience and feel. Your ability to feel the existence of beyond-human spiritual power is negligible. Also, you will find it difficult to connect with anything or anyone in your life. High levels of skepticism, excessive need for sensual pleasures, and overly attached to materialistic needs are clear signs of an unbalanced and blocked Sahasrara. Miracle workers and empaths generally see muddy and dark traits in your aura if you have a problem with your crown chakra.

Physical symptoms of an unbalanced crown chakra could include multi-system failures and paralysis too. Numerous genetic disorders are believed to be karmically connected to compromised energy flow in the crown chakra. Meditation on the divine light is a great tool to open up, clear and balance your crown chakra and its energy field. Use these steps for meditating on the divine light.

- Sit in a comfortable meditation posture, preferably cross-legged on the floor. Your back should be erect, and your body should be relaxed but alert.

- Your hands should be on your lap with your left hand above your right, and your palms facing upward. This is the mudra of receiving energy from the universe.

- Close your eyes and breathe slowly and relaxedly. Focus your thoughts on the crown chakra on top of your head.

- Visualize a streak of bright white light entering you through the crown chakra. Feel this light spiraling and descending into your body.

- Feel and experience the visualization of the warm glow of this light as it gently engulfs you. Imagine every cell of your body being permeated by this light. Imagine your mind is filled with this divine light and consciousness.

- You can repeat any or all of these affirmations:

  - I feel the power and protection of the universal divine light.

  - This divine power protects and nourishes me.

  - I always walk in this divine light.

  - I feel empowered and stronger in this divine light.

In this state, intuitive thoughts and inspirations can enter your body and mind. Give this for these powerful elements as you feel them entering your consciousness. You could think of another person bathed in this divine light instead of yourself. You can repeat the affirmations mentioned above by replacing the person's name instead of "I." When you feel satisfied with the meditation, offer your thanks, and open your eyes gently.

Sit in this position for about 5-10 minutes each day, allowing yourself to be bathed in and cleansed by the divine light. Remember, this divine light is a manifestation of your higher self. It represents the peace that lies beyond the human realm and consciousness.

Working with All Your Chakras Together

This section is dedicated to giving you a meditation session with which you can energize and balance all your chakras right from the root up to the crown, one at a time. Take this exercise slowly and confidently after you have learned how to handle each of your seven chakras separately. Slow but steady is the key element of success in energizing and cleansing your chakras. Typically, this entire exercise could take anywhere up to 10 minutes.

Root chakra - Sit cross-legged on the floor. Let the tips of your forefinger and thumb (of both hands) touch each other gently. Place your hands gently against your knees in the sitting position. Focus on the root chakra's location, imagining a large red dot there. Chant the bija mantra LAM silently thinking about the chakra and its power to help you survive and keep you stable and strong.

Contract and hold your perineum as long as you can. As you do so, think of a red flower bud and visualize an aura of red energy emanating from it. Visualize that as the energy emanates, the bud opens up and becomes a full-bloomed flower with all its petals filled with energy. When you feel satisfied, move on to the sacral chakra exercise.

A good way of checking if you are satisfied and ready to move to the next chakra is to look out for a sense of being "clean" at each energy center at which stage you are ready to move to the next.

Sacral chakra - Sit on your knees, rather than being cross-legged for this. Your back should be straight but relaxed. Place your hands on your lap, left hand beneath the right, palms facing upward, and the thumb tips touching each other gently. Focus on the location of your sacral chakra (imagining an orange ball of fire at the place) and silently, but clearly, chant the bija mantra, VAM.

As you chant, recall the value and importance of this chakra and how it can affect your life positively. Repeat this for as long as you can. At the end of a satisfactory sacral chakra focus, once you feel a sense of being "clean," move on to the next chakra, the solar plexus.

Solar plexus chakra - For this too, sit on your knees and keep your back straight and relaxed. Put your hands in front of your navel. Join the fingers in the form of a prayer pose and point the fingertips away from you. Make sure the fingers are straight, and the thumbs are crossed. Imagine a ball of yellow at the location of your solar plexus chakra and focus on the value of this energy center in your life even as you silently but clearly chant the bija mantra, RAM. When you are ready, move on to the next, namely the heart chakra.

Heart chakra - Sit cross-legged and place your left hand on the left knee and the right hand in front of your heart. The tips of the thumb and forefinger of both hands should touch each other gently. Focus on the heart chakra, imagining a green ball of light in the location. Chant the bija mantra of the heart, YAM, silently but clearly.

Allow the thoughts regarding the heart chakra to fill your mind. Think of its importance to your life and how it can affect you and those around you. Sit like this until you feel satisfied and get that sense of being "clean." Typically, the sense of being clean intensifies as you move upwards from chakra to chakra.

Throat chakra - For the throat chakra, sit on your knees and intertwine the fingers of both hands in the inward direction so the fingertips point toward you. The two thumbs must touch each other at the tip and must point in the upward direction. Imagine a ball of light blue light or a gentle fire in your throat and chant the bija mantra, HAM.

Think of the throat chakra, its functions, and its impact on your life. After about five minutes, you will feel the sense of "cleanliness" intensifying. You can now move to the third eye chakra.

Third eye or brow chakra - Sit cross-legged comfortably. Bring your hands together and bend them all except the middle finger. The middle fingertips should touch each other and point outward, and the rest of the four fingers must touch each other at the point of bend and point inward. Place your hands in this position near the lower part of your breast area.

Focus on the third eye chakra by imagining a ball of indigo light in the location. Think about all the strengths of this energy center and the positive impact it can have on your life, even as you chant the bija mantra, AUM. When you feel satisfied, you can move on to the crown chakra.

Crown chakra - Sit cross-legged and place your hand on your stomach. The tips of your little fingers must touch each other gently and should be pointed away from you and in the upward direction. Cross the other four fingers, ensuring the right thumb is resting on the left thumb.

In this position, chant the bija mantra of the crown chakra, SOHAM, or AUM or NG, thinking of a purple ball of light on top of your head. Recall the importance and value of the crown chakra in your life and how it can help you lead a more meaningful and interconnected life with others. When you feel the sense of "cleanliness" intensified, you can open your eyes. You will feel your body and mind completely relaxed at this stage.

Opening up your chakras fully is a long but highly rewarding process. When the energy centers in your body are totally balanced, and the energy flows through your nadis freely, without blockages and you can feel the positivity in your life. Your ability to handle the outcomes of Kundalini Awakening increases multifold.

Chapter 5: Psychic Abilities and the Third Eye

One particular chakra, the third eye chakra, requires a little more focus than the rest because it is connected with the "sixth sense" and psychic powers. Therefore, a separate chapter dedicated to the Ajna Chakra makes sense here to enhance your ability to handle Kundalini Awakening when it happens.

To reiterate, the third eye chakra is located at the center of the forehead, right between the eyes. The color associated with this energy center is indigo or royal blue. It is the seat of our psychic powers. It regulates and controls our psychic powers so we can receive and transfer information to the realms beyond the planes of human consciousness. It is the seat of our internal intuition, and when fully developed, can read the past, present, and future accurately. A person with a well-developed Ajna Chakra can interact and get guidance from the spirit realm and from loved ones who have crossed over.

The Ajna Chakra is also an effective and powerful manifestation tool. We can use it to visualize our dreams and hopes and harness the universal power to manifest them in our life. When we visualize our dreams, it is more than just our imagination working. It sees our desires through our inner eye.

Interestingly, the Ajna Chakra is closely connected to the solar plexus chakra or our "gut feeling." When these two energy centers are aligned with each other and work synchronously, our life can turn out meaningful and fulfilling. The synchronized energy of the two centers can help us understand and harness our intuitive powers so we can overcome our challenges and difficulties easily.

With an open and balanced third eye chakra, we have improved clarity and focus along with a powerful intuition. Here are basic tips to activate, strengthen, and balance the third eye chakra and the energy it holds:

- Practice visualization and meditation regularly, both guided and simple breathing types.
- Try to include royal blue and indigo into your life, whether in the clothes you buy, the colors you paint, the jewelry you choose, or anything else.
- Holding or wearing gemstones like Lapis Lazuli, Tanzanite, Amethyst, Apatite, and Labradorite help to enhance your meditation experience.
- Work with Tarot Cards and other forms and conduits of oracles.
- Massage the area of your third eye with our essential oils like myrrh, sandalwood, etc.
- Don't forget to give daily thanks to your third eye and its power to help you lead a happy, fulfilling life.

Opening the Third Eye Chakra

Keeping the third eye open and energy flow as free-flowing as possible is essential to not only harness your spiritual powers but also to return safely and sanely from those realms beyond human consciousness, a common outcome of Kundalini Awakening. These strategies have known to work magical wonders to open the third eye and keep its energy balanced and unblocked.

Cultivate Silence - Learn to foster the silence of your mind. For an average human, the mind is a cacophony of thoughts and ideas that threaten to take our world by storm. Not only this, but these thoughts also create a lot of noise in our minds. Our ability to hear and interpret the messages that come to us from the higher and subtler realms get lost in the noise.

The third eye chakra can go to that "in-between" space to collect and get guidance and messages from the spirits of the other world. In the presence of noise, you cannot hear the messages. Therefore, it is imperative you cultivate silence of the mind and learn to handle overwhelming thoughts.

You can use a variety of ways to calm and silence your mind, including meditation, indulging in your favorite hobby or art, or simply sitting calmly in the midst of nature doing nothing but observing the surrounding beauty.

Hone your intuitive powers - we all are endowed with intuitive powers. The problem is these powers need to be continuously honed and sharpened for them to be effectively used. Not using them regularly dulls our intuition, and we get disconnected from our inner voice that receives and passes on messages from the outer world. The sharper your intuition is, the more powerful your third eye chakra becomes. Here are simple ways to connect with and hone your intuition:

First, recognize how and when your intuition speaks to you. Usually, intuition is not loud and clear like a human voice. Instead, it sends subtle messages through slow-moving or flashes of imagery. Often, you will talk with your intuition, wondering how to get clarity about the received message.

Sometimes, the messages come in goosebumps, an uncomfortable feeling in the gut, a sour taste in your mouth, or a sense of inexplicable relief. Often, the messages could come as an emotion. For example, you intuitively like or hate someone you've just met.

This could be your intuition, sending you a message about this person.

Just be alert to subtle forms of messages that your body and mind send you. To do that, you must connect with and talk with your inner voice. With practice, you will realize that you can easily catch on to the subtlest of hints that your intuition is trying to give you.

Try to connect with your intuition daily - Keep aside a dedicated time to connect with your intuition daily. Give time and effort to your intuitive powers and see what they are trying to tell you. This is especially important when you have to make a critical decision. However, to ensure you can understand your intuition's language, it is imperative you talk with it every day.

Take small decisions, too, after consulting with your intuition. It could be something as seemingly mundane as which dress to wear each morning. Stand in front of your wardrobe for a little while and ask your intuition which dress would suit you best today. Then, calm your mind, and look out for signs and signals it might be sending to you. Like this, try to connect with your intuition daily.

Write down what you felt or experienced when you tried connecting with your intuition. Don't leave it to your memory, at least in the initial stages of your learning experience. Write down what you felt, your thoughts, and everything else when you sat down each day and connect with your intuition. The more practice you get, the better your skills will become.

Meditate as often as you can; the deeper your connection is with your intuition, the easier it will be to read and interpret its messages. Meditation is an excellent tool to deepen your connection with your intuitive powers. Meditation teaches you to clear your mind and recognize the subtle impulses and signs that your intuition is trying to give you.

And finally, learn to trust yourself and your intuitive powers. The more faith you have in your powers, the better outcomes you will get.

Trust yourself because no one loves you more than you do. No one wants to see you happy and successful more than you do.

Build your creativity skills - each one of us is born with creativity. It is up to us to nurture, nourish and develop it to achieve our full potential. Creativity is a useful tool to eliminate rational fears and crutches that hold you down when you are, in reality, powerful to soar high in the clouds.

When your rational mind is relegated to the background, then the mental chatter also reduces, helping to achieve calmness needed to communicate with your intuitive powers. Also, when you can calm that part of your mind that wants to take charge of your life, then you are effectively opening up numerous opportunities for yourself. Your third eye chakra has increased space to unfold, grow, and blossom.

How can you nurture your creativity? Here are tips to help your creativity grow and blossom:

- Invest your time and energy on hobbies and activities that energize you and make you happy. Learn a new craft or art. It is not important to be perfect in what you do. The trick is to let your inspiration flow through your mind into your hands. Be ready to be surprised when you allow your creativity to flow unhindered.

- Experiment with creativity. You need not have a perfect plan. Just do anything that requires your creativity to flow through. For a simple example, just buy yourself an adult coloring book, and experiment with colors. Or make a palette of watercolors and simply splash them around on a piece of paper and observe the results. Or put on some music and dance to it as if no one is looking at you.

- Get sufficient nourishment for your body through nutritious food, restful sleep, and a good amount of physical activity.

- Invest in yourself. Do something once a week that is only for you. It could be something as simple as a visit to the local art gallery or sipping a cup of morning tea by yourself, or an afternoon curled up in bed with your favorite book, or anything else. This alone time will give you a deep sense of calmness and also allow you to connect with yourself and your intuitive powers.

• Spend some time with nature. Take a walk in the park. Or take a hike to a place close to your home. Look for and find an opportunity to spend time with nature.

Ground Yourself to Soar Fearlessly - It is an ironic truth that to soar fearlessly, we must plant both our feet firmly on the ground. In the same way, to open our third eye, our root chakra should be strong and robust, giving you the needed sense of stability and strength with the support of which you can soar fearlessly. Your root chakra forms the firm foundation over which you can build your life that takes you on wondrous flights outside the human realm. The root chakra is what brings you back home.

Also, the information that comes into our body and mind when our third eye is opened could be unfamiliar, unusual, and difficult to digest for common minds. Therefore, you must first energize and empower your tangible body and mind, and only when you are ready can you tackle the power of the subtle universe.

Chapter 6: Kundalini Yoga: Asanas and Pranayama

Now that you know the importance and have practiced the skills of meditation and energizing and balancing your chakras, you can initiate yourself into the actual Kundalini Yoga designed to awaken the sleeping but highly potent Kundalini. Let us start by understanding Kundalini Yoga in a bit more detail.

What is Kundalini Yoga?

In the early stages of understanding energy in the universe, Kundalini was seen as a science and study of spiritual philosophy and energy. In ancient times, especially in India, kings and their royal families were mandated to sit with Kundalini masters to learn, understand, and master Kundalini teachings and the way of its spiritual visions.

Yogi Bhajan is credited with bringing this highly intelligent yet compassionate form of Yoga to the west. He combined the power of ancient wisdom with modern practicality and made sure Kundalini Yoga was accessible to everyone who was interested in empowering themselves with its power. The regular practice of Kundalini Yoga will help you in these ways:

- It helps you achieve boundless love, lightness of living and joy.

- You learn of your body's geometry.

- You will understand, and therefore be able to alter suitably and efficiently, the way your emotions, energy and motions work in your body and mind.

- It helps you clear energy blockages in your body and ensures the flow of vital energy is free and full.

- It helps you create a mind-body connection to its full potential.

- Kundalini Yoga will help to pull the coiled snake from its sleeping position and transfer the energy through the spine right up to the top of your head. The energy is also radiated outward so it can flow and balance your chakras all across your body.

Elements of Kundalini Yoga

Kundalini Yoga combines breath, mudras, mantras, and kriyas to awaken the Kundalini.

Importance of Breath in Kundalini Yoga - The most common form of breathing exercise used in Kundalini Yoga is the Long Deep Breathing. However, there are many other yoga postures and breathing techniques used too. Critically, you must know that every yoga kriya and breathing technique in Kundalini Yoga has a specific process aimed at releasing or balancing specific energy.

For example, in the Long Deep Breathing exercise, you will need to place your hands specifically on your heart and stomach. Another example, the Breath of Fire, is a common and popular breathing technique in Kundalini Yoga. It is practiced through a process of rapid breathing consisting of equal parts of inhalation and exhalation through the nostrils and by "pumping out" air from the stomach. This technique helps to create an increased level of oxygen flow in your bloodstream and also charges the electromagnetic field around you.

Importance of Mantras in Kundalini Yoga - Mantras are not mere words strung together for aural beauty. Yes, they do sound musically beautiful. However, mantras go beyond that. They have the power to create chemical reactions in your brain to positively affect your moods and experiences in life.

For example, our moods, like happiness, joy, sadness, etc. result from vibrations of varying frequencies. By chanting a specific mantra, you are effectively creating a chemical situation in the brain that results in a particular frequency, which, in turn, results in affecting your mood according to your desire.

Chanting mantras drives your body to vibrate at particular frequencies (depending on the mantra). Consequently, your mood is elevated to higher vibrations resulting in creating a happy and abundant state of mind. To give you an illustration, HAR (sounds like "hud") is a mantra that brings in prosperity and success.

Mantras need not be chanted only in a sitting position. You can chant them when lying down or driving or waiting in line for something or anywhere else that proves convenient. However, when you sit and chant the mantra, you also harness the power of meditation.

Importance of Kriyas in Kundalini Yoga - Breath, sound, and posture together form the kriya. Kriya in Sanskrit translates to "action." In Kundalini Yoga, kriya is a set of exercises consisting of specific actions, breathing mechanisms, and poses that are designed for a specific manifestation in your life. The effect of kriya is felt on all levels of the body, mind and spirit resulting in abundant and fulfilling life. For example, there is a kriya for balancing your aura which is highly effective to protect your energy field, elevate your energy levels and boost your stamina.

Importance of Mudras in Kundalini Yoga - Mudras, as you already know, are hand positions and gestures that include locking of fingers, touching fingertips, etc., so you can direct the focused energy on the required part of your body. In mudras, finger to finger placement is a common mechanism, and pressing it down will activate and release energy.

For example, the "Gyan Mudra" is one of the most common ones used in Kundalini Yoga. This mudra brings together the tips of your thumb and forefinger to stimulate knowledge. "Gyan" in Sanskrit translates to knowledge.

Importance of Meditations in Kundalini Yoga - In Kundalini Yoga, meditation sessions help to release energy and heal damaged energy fields. During and after a meditation session, you tend to feel heightened, more aware, more stimulated, and more awakened than before. The meditation sessions have varying lengths, depending on the desired outcomes.

For example, a three-minute meditation will positively affect the blood circulation system in your body and the electromagnetic field around you. An 11-minute session can affect your glandular and nervous systems, whereas a 31-minute session can affect every cell and tissue in your body and leave you feeling light and rejuvenated, ready to take on the world.

Common Asanas in Kundalini Yoga

This section is dedicated to giving you some common and easy-to-do Kundalini Yoga asanas. So, let's get started.

Sukhasana - In Sanskrit, Sukhasana means "easy pose." This is a very simple pose that you can use for all your breathing meditation. Cross your legs at the ankles or place both your feet on the ground. Press the lower spine forward so your back is erect yet relaxed.

Siddhasana - Translating to "Perfect Pose," Siddhasana is considered the most comfortable asana and is also believed to promote psychic powers. To do this asana, sit cross-legged in the following way:

• Let your right heel press against your right perineum (the anal bone)

- Let your right sole press against your left thigh.

- Place the left heel over the right heel and press that part of your body just above the genitals.

- The toes of both feet must be tucked into the groove formed between the thighs and the calves.

- Knees should be on the ground.

Padmasana - Commonly called the "Lotus Pose," ("Padma" in Sanskrit translates to "lotus"), this asana is one of the most popular and powerful poses for meditations. Again, you must sit cross-legged using these tips:

- Lift your left foot and place it on the upper part of the right thigh.

- Then lift your right foot and place it on the upper part of the left thigh.

- Try to keep your feet as close to your body as possible.

When you see pictures of this asana, it might look simple, however, it takes a lot of practice to get it right. It is believed to have the power to enhance deep meditation and was commonly practiced by ancient Hindu yogis. Remember to keep the right leg always on top.

Vajrasana - Called the "Rock Pose," uses the following steps for the Vajrasana pose:

- Kneel down.

- Then sit on your heels by allowing the tops of your feet to touch the ground.

- The heels should press the nerves in the middle of your buttocks.

There is an interesting reason as to why this is called the "rock pose." The ancient yogis believed that this asana empowers the practitioner to even digest rocks.

Camel Pose - Excellent for opening the heart chakra, the camel pose stimulates the nervous system because it creates maximum compression of your spine. It also improves the flexibility of your neck and spine. It stretches the abdominal muscles, the throat energy center and the throat muscles, and also adjusts the reproductive organs. Here are the steps to do the camel pose:

- Kneel on the ground with your thighs and knees perpendicular to the floor.
- Arch back and hold on to your ankles.
- Let your head fall back fully.
- Push your hips forward.
- Do long, deep breathing.

Locust Pose - Lie on your stomach. Your feet must be together, and your chin should touch the ground. Place your fists under the thigh and hip joint. Slowly, raise your legs and thighs up. Ensure your legs are together. Breathe long and deep.

Baby Pose - Sit on your heels. Slowly bring the forehead forward to touch the ground. Arms should be relaxed at the sides of your body with the palms facing upward.

Celibate Pose - Also called the "Hero Pose," the Celibate Pose is designed to channelize sexual energy up the spine. For this pose, keep your feet apart to the width of your hips. Kneel and sit between the feet.

Common Pranayama Techniques in Kundalini Yoga

Kundalini Yoga employs a wide range of pranayama techniques to harness the power of the breath to effectively reach and manage various higher states of consciousness, leading to overall well-being. Here are some of the most common and popular pranayama techniques used in Kundalini Yoga.

Long Deep Breathing - This pranayama exercise is an excellent tool to balance your emotions, calm your mind, and bring your body, mind, and spirit into harmonious alignment. It is one of the most important and commonly practiced pranayama techniques in Kundalini Yoga. The benefits and importance of Long Deep Breathing are:

- As it impacts your parasympathetic nervous system, this breathing technique relaxes and calms you.

- It prevents and reduces toxin accumulation in your body as it helps in clearing even the small-sized air sacs (or alveoli) in your lungs. This breathing technique also fills the lungs to their full capacity even while readjusting your magnetic field to your advantage.

- It increases the strength and flow of prana Vayu.

- Stimulates endorphin production, a hormone known to help in fighting depression.

- Enhances the pumping of the spinal fluid to the brain resulting in greater energy for the brain.

- Enhances the alertness of your brain.

- Improves the function of the pituitary gland, an important element to positively affect your intuitive powers.

- It enhances your ability to deal with stress, thereby improving physical and emotional healing.

- Empowers you to manage negativity, including negative emotions.

Here are the steps needed for beginners to perform the Long Deep Breathing technique.

The inhalation and exhalation processes are divided into three parts of breathing. When you breathe in:

1. Fill your abdomen with air first

2. Then expand your chest

3. And last, lift the clavicle and the upper ribs.

When you breathe out, use the reverse direction.

1. First, contract the clavicle and upper ribs area

2. Then your chest area

3. And finally, your abdomen so that all the air is pushed out of your body.

In the final stage of the exhalation, when you empty your stomach, you will notice that the navel point pushes back toward the spine. Also, for beginners, it is a good idea to lie down in the initial days of practicing Long Deep Breathing. Place your left hand on your stomach and your right hand on the chest so you can feel the movement of air and the expansions in the parts of your body.

Let us look at the three parts of long deep breathing in detail:

Abdominal breathing - First, allow your breathing to settle at a relaxed and normal pace. When you are ready, focus on your navel. Take a slow and deep breath and allow your belly to expand in a relaxed manner. When you exhale, pull the navel back towards your spine and move it up. Keep the chest relaxed and use only your abdomen for breathing here.

Chest breathing - For this, you have to sit straight and keep the diaphragm still. Do not allow your abdomen to expand as you breathe in. Use only your chest muscles while inhaling. Do it slowly and feel the chest muscles expand. Also, you will notice that the ribs at the bottom move a lot more than the top ones. Compare the chest breathing technique with the abdominal breathing technique.

Clavicular breathing - Sit straight and keep your abdomen relaxed and your navel slightly pulled in. Now lift your chest without breathing. Now breathe in slowly and expand your shoulders and the collarbone or clavicle. Keep the chest in the lifted position and exhale.

Now, long deep breathing combines all these breathing techniques. Let us put them together. Each part of the three expansions is distinct and separate. When you combine all three, you get the long deep breathing technique. Start the inhalation using the abdominal breathing. Add the chest breath, and finally, the clavicular breathing.

When you have mastered the technique, you can do all three in a seamless, smooth flow.

Breath of Fire - This breathing technique is continuous, rapid, and rhythmic. You inhale and exhale quickly and in equal intervals with no pause. Target about 2-3 cycles per second.

- The mouth should be closed, and your breathing should be through the nostrils.

- This exercise is powerful from the solar plexus energy center or the navel.

- During inhalation, the muscles in the upper abdomen relax, and the diaphragm goes down.

- During exhalation, you must expel air powerfully through the nose by pushing the navel and the solar plexus back toward your spine.

- The chest is relaxed, though slightly lifted throughout the exercise.

You can start this exercise for a duration of 1-3 minutes. As you get comfortable with the exercise, you can increase the duration. Typically, about 10 minutes daily of the Breath of Fire technique will do wonders for your Kundalini.

Alternate Nostril Breathing - This is a very simple, yet powerful pranayama technique used often by Kundalini practitioners, both novices and the experienced. It helps to create a deep sense of harmony and well-being on emotional, physical and mental levels. It integrates all your energy centers and also helps to ground you. It also balanced the left and right hemispheres of your brain.

- Use the easy pose (Sukhasana) or sit on a chair for this meditation.

- Use your thumb and forefingers of your right hand to create a U. The thumb should be over the right nostril and the index finger for the left nostril.

- Close your left nostril with the index finger and inhale through your right nostril.

- At the end of the inhalation, close the right nostril with your thumb and exhale through your left nostril.

- Now, inhale through your left nostril and exhale through your right nostril.

Repeat this exercise for about 3-5 minutes. To end it, breathe for a few seconds, hold your breath, bring down your hand, and exhale.

Chapter 7: Kundalini Yoga: Mantras and Mudras

This chapter is all about the mantras and mudras used in Kundalini Yoga. So, let's get to it straight away.

What are Mantras?

Mantras are not just words strung together to form a nice-sounding sound. They go beyond simple recitation and singing. They have the power to work on the subtle aspects of your being because of the arrangement of syllables in the mantras.

The tongue moves as we speak, sing, or recite the mantras (or sacred words), right? As we do this, we hit several important nerve points in our palate, which, in turn, sends the required messages to our brain to do the things we are praying for. Mantras have been set by some of the original humans and need not be understood for you to harness their power. Mantras are pure sounds with the power to stimulate the brain and the world to do our bidding.

For example, the words "Ong" or "Maa" are not created or limited to one language. All humans are born with these sounds and utterances. The repeated chanting of these mantras drives the brain to do our bidding. Mantras are so powerful that you can control your body and mind with them, provided you repeat them accurately for enough times.

Mantras have the power to help you shift your moods, your habits, and your entire lifestyle. The challenge is to be consistent, diligent and committed to the chanting of the mantras regularly and unfailingly. Let us look at the mantras commonly used in Kundalini Yoga.

Mantras are typically in Gurmukhi, an ancient Indian script. However, thanks to introducing Kundalini Yoga to the western world, some mantras are occasionally available in English too. You have been introduced to certain bija mantras of the seven chakras. These mantras are excellent tools to activate and balance the energy of the chakras.

Kundalini Yoga Mantras (Utterances)

Let us go a little deeper into more Kundalini Yoga mantras.

The Adi Mantra - Adi in Sanskrit translates to "first" or "primary." Therefore, the Adi Mantra is the first or primary mantra in Kundalini Yoga. It goes like this: Ong Namo Guru dev Namo.

The meaning of the Adi Mantra is "I salute and pay my respects to Creative Wisdom and to the divine teacher within." This mantra is specifically used to tune in to the divine flow of self-knowledge lying latent within each of us. Ideally, you must chant this mantra three times before and after you do any asana, meditation, kriya, etc.

The Truth Mantra - It goes like this: Sat Nam. It means "I am the truth" or 'truth is my identity." This mantra reinforces the existence of divine consciousness in each of us. Interestingly, Kundalini and other yogic practitioners use this mantra as a way of greeting each other and also as a meditative mantra. A classic way of using this mantra goes: While you inhale, say "Sat" and while you exhale, say "Nam."

The Humility Mantra - The mantra is, "Guru Guru Wahe Guru Guru Ram Das Guru," and it translates into "Wise, wise is the person who serves the Infinite and the Limitless." This mantra calls on the spirit of Guru Ram Das, the fourth Guru of Sikhism, who was known for his immense patience, humility and compassion. To chant his mantra:

- Sit in the easy pose. Keep your hands anywhere you feel comfortable; on your lap, on your knees, or anywhere else.
- Close your eyes and gently focus on your third eye.

Now chant the mantra slowly. You can sing it or say it in a monotone. It would be great if you could complete one recitation during one breath.

The Guru Mantra - The Guru Mantra goes like this, "Wahe Guru." While the number of words appears to be just two, the meaning and translation of it covers the entire universal divine power. The translation of this mantra is, "I feel ecstatic when I know and experience Divine Wisdom." This mantra reflects the ecstasy you feel when you move from darkness to light (ultimate knowledge). This mantra is the infinite teacher of the soul. Many kriyas of Kundalini Yoga use this mantra.

Also, another translation of the mantra is, "I am healthy. I am holy." Therefore, this mantra reflects our birthright to health, happiness and sacredness.

The Mangala Charn Mantra - This mantra is a powerful tool to clear the doubts in our minds and opens us up for guidance and protection from the universal power. The mantra is:

Aad Guray Nameh

Jugad Guray Nameh

Sat Guray Nameh

Siri Guru Devay Nameh

The translation of the Mangala Charn Mantra is:

I salute the primal wisdom.

I salute the wisdom of the ages.

I salute true wisdom.

I salute the great invisible wisdom.

The Mantra for Bounty and Prosperity - This mantra is in English and goes like this, "I am blissful, bountiful, and beautiful." This mantra reminds you that you are made in the mold of the universal divine power, and therefore, you be nothing but beautiful. The divine power, which many of us call God, made us perfect, putting all our features in the right places. For example, what if He had put our knees where our ears are or our mouth where our stomach is located. This mantra reminds us of this perfection of our body.

We are bountiful because we have everything we need. To understand the power of bounty, you simply need to ask a blind man the value of sight, a deaf man the value of sound, a crippled man the value of healthy limbs, etc. When we understand the inadequacies faced by these people, we realize how bountiful we are.

We are blissful because we are alive and well despite all the sufferings and pain we undergo, and despite all the wrongs we commit, wittingly or unwittingly. Imagine how many mistakes you have made, and yet you remain in one piece. Isn't that a reason to feel blissful? Therefore, this mantra reminds us of the bounty, beauty, and bliss we have. This mantra is also great for self-esteem and confidence building.

The Siri Mantra or the Magic Mantra - The Magic Mantra has the power to remove all negativity and obstacles from your life. This mantra is:

Ek Ong Kar Sat Gur Prasad, Sat Gur Prasad Ek Ong Kar

The translation of this mantra is something like this:

"The Divine Being and I are one; I know this by the Grace of the wise and true Guru.

I know this by the Grace of the wise and true Guru, The Divine Being and I are one."

Repeating this mantra is excellent to improve your intuitive powers too. After you have mastered the power of this mantra, anything you say gets amplified. Therefore, you should pay attention to positive talk and avoid negative talks. However, it is equally important to know that if this mantra is not chanted correctly, then it can backfire on you. Therefore, it would be a good idea to meditate and learn to calm your mind before beginning this chant.

Kundalini Yoga Mudras (Hand Postures and Gestures)

The power in and of our hands goes beyond the basic functionalities of work. They have it in them to be an energy map of our health and consciousness. Each area and portion of the hand is related to a certain body part and to different thoughts and emotions.

By touching, curling, stretching and crossing your palms and fingers, you are effectively communicating with your body and mind. Hand positions and gestures are called mudras in Sanskrit. It is a technique used by yogis and Kundalini Yoga practitioners to send clear messages to our body-mind system of energy.

Let us look at some important mudras used in Kundalini Yoga:

In the hand mudra, your thumb is you (or your ego), and it connects to different planets depending on the finger which your thumb touches.

Gyan Mudra - Referred to as the Seal of Knowledge, this stimulates calmness, wisdom, knowledge and receptivity. Gently touch the tip of your thumb and index finger, keep the other three fingers straight, and you have the Gyan Mudra. The Gyan Mudra is ruled by Jupiter, the planet known for its powers of expansion and growth.

Shuni Mudra - Known as the Seal of Patience and Courage, this mudra is an excellent tool to build patience, commitment, and discernment skills. This mudra requires you to touch the tip of the thumb and the middle finger with each other, and keep the other three fingers straight. The master of this mudra is Saturn, the planet known to be a hard taskmaster, and teaches us the importance of taking responsibility and doing our duty courageously and righteously.

Ravi or Surya Mudra - Known as the Seal of Life, Energy, or Sun, the Surya Mudra is great for building the strength of your nerves, revitalizing your energy, and for overall good health. For this mudra, touch the tip of your thumb and the ring (or third) finger together, keeping the other three fingers straight. The planet master of this mudra is the Sun, famous for its power to improve sexuality, energy, and health. It is also ruled by Planet Uranus responsible for nerve strength, intuitive powers, and adaptability to change.

Buddhi Mudra - Referred to as the Seal of Mental Clarity, this mudra promotes clear and intuitive communication. It also promotes psychic development, along with helping you improve your oratory and communication skills. The mudra is formed by touching the tip of your thumb and the little finger, leaving the other three straight. The planet of the Buddhi Mudra is Mercury, which is known for its quickness and mental powers.

Pranam Mudra - Commonly called the Prayer Pose, this mudra seamlessly combines the negative side of the body, which is the left or the feminine side, with the positive side of the body on the right, masculine side resulting in a balanced effect on the person. This mudra consists of touching the palms with all the fingers of both hands completely.

The Pranam Mudra has a scientific reasoning behind it. There is a difference in polarity between the right and left side, or the Pingala and the Ida, respectively. When the right and left hands come together and touch each other, the polarities are neutralized, creating a neutral space in the electromagnetic field.

In the Pranam Mudra position, the knuckles of the thumbs touch the notch of the breastbone. This place is an important reflex point for the vagus nerve, an important nerve that goes up to the pineal gland from the front part of your body. A lot of research has been conducted on the vagus nerve, and the observations show it plays an important role in feelings of goodness, compassion and empathy.

The Pranam mudra creates pressure at this reflex point and drives the pituitary and the pineal glands to increase their secretions, which results in resonance in the brain. Your consciousness moves from the normal rhythmic state to a meditative state, ensuring that your prayers come straight from the heart. This is the scientific reason behind why we fold our hands during prayer.

Venus Lock - This mudra promotes improved concentration, glandular balance and also improves sexual energy. For men, this mudra requires the fingers of the two hands to be interlaced with the left little finger being right at the bottom. The left thumb is placed between the soft webbed region between the thumb and index finger of the right hand. The right thumb is placed over the left thumb at the mound found at its base.

For women, it is the same thing except that the right and left thumb positions are interchanged. The mounds at the base of the thumbs represent Venus, the planet of sexuality and sensuality. The thumb represents your ego.

Chapter 8: Kundalini Yoga: Kriyas (Full Sequences)

You have been introduced to the basic meaning of kriya, which is a set of mudras, pranayama, and asana exercises. Let us look a little deeper into some of the most common and important kriyas practiced in Kundalini Yoga.

There are thousands of kriyas designed for the awakening of the Kundalini. We will look at some from a beginner's perspective. However, before you start on your kriya practice, it is important to read, understand and follow this set of guidelines.

Guidelines for the Practice of Kriyas

Use these basic guidelines to follow before, during, and after, a kriya session.

Before the practice:

• All distractions like mobiles and electronic devices should be turned off.

• Eat a light snack along with water about two to three hours before the session.

- Wear comfortable, loose-fitting clothes. Also, wear a head covering like a scarf, bandana, etc. Make sure all your clothes and garments are made of natural fibers because they are excellent insulators to keep you grounded during meditation.

- Have a blanket or sheet made of natural fiber like wool or cotton to sit on. You also need a second sheet or shawl to cover yourself during relaxation and meditation periods.

- If you have a problem with your lower back, legs, or hips, then you can use a small cushion to sit in an elevated position when seated or during meditation.

During the practice:

- The first and foremost purpose of Kundalini Yoga is to increase your self-awareness. Therefore, tune in to your body signals, listen to them, and follow what they say.

- Challenge yourself to do just a little more than you believe you can. For example, if you think that you cannot sit for over five minutes for your meditation, push yourself to sit for 6 minutes.

- Stick to the instructions given for each kriya strictly. Ensure you follow the order and the type of posture, asana, and breathing technique suggested for each kriya.

- Do not try to do a kriya beyond the recommended maximum time. You can shorten the period if you wish. However, remember to reduce the time proportionally for all the elements of the kriya.

- When you are in a class with your instructor, please clear your doubts about any aspect of the kriya. Getting the kriyas right is important for the success of Kundalini Awakening.

- You can drink water, if needed, between the exercises.

For women, during the heavy parts of your monthly menstruation time, avoid doing strenuous yoga. Particularly, avoid the Breath of Fire breathing technique, Camel Pose, Stretch Pose, Locust Pose,

Root Lock, etc. Instead of actually performing such strenuous exercises during heavy periods, you can simply visualize yourself doing them or ask your instructor for a modified version suitable for you during that period.

After the practice:

• Drink plenty of water.

• Tune in to your physical, emotional and mental state of mind and try to observe what they are trying to tell you.

• Try to incorporate at least one simple exercise learned in the class into your daily life. For example, if you have learned the Long Deep Breathing technique well, then you could try it during any free time during the day.

The Sat Kriya

This is the fundamental kriya in Kundalini Yoga, and you should do this kriya in a 3-minute session at least three times a day. There are multiple benefits of doing this kriya, including improved overall general health, improved heart health, etc. Even if you don't have time for any other kriya, do this one to keep your body clean, relaxed, and healthy. Use these steps for this kriya:

• Sit using the Rock Pose.

• Stretch your arms over your head. Elbows should be straight until your forearms hug your ears or the sides of your head.

• Your spine should be straight and still. Make sure you don't feel a pelvic thrust or a spinal flex.

• Leaving out the index fingers, interlace all your fingers. The tips of the index fingers must touch each other and should be pointed upward. Women should cross the left thumb over the right. Men should cross the right thumb over the left.

• The above position should be maintained throughout the kriya.

- Begin chanting the Sat Nam Mantra rhythmically, repeating about every 10 seconds for 8 minutes.

- As you breathe in and pull your navel toward your spine, say "Sat" and feel the pressure on your third eye.

- Say "Nam" as you exhale and relax your belly muscles.

- As you get into this rhythm, your belly and greater abdomen muscles begin to move rhythmically, and you will notice that your breath is automatically controlled.

- To end the kriya, inhale and gently squeeze your sphincter muscles and feel the energy rising up your spine.

- Hold it for a little while and focus on your crown chakra. Now, exhale.

- Breathe in and out gently and open your eyes.

The Stretch Pose

The Stretch Pose is uniquely and commonly used in Kundalini Yoga. Yes, it is slightly challenging but highly worthy and rewarding. The Stretch Pose stimulates and activities the third eye chakra and also affects the entire body. The activation of the third eye chakra boosts self-esteem and resolve.

This kriya uses the navel as a fulcrum to strengthen the muscles in the abdomen and reset the entire nervous system. When used along with the Breath of Fire, it has the power to calm and rejuvenate your body and mind even as your blood is purified and energized. The benefits of the Stretch Pose include:

- Strengthens your navel point, which is your power center.

- Strengthens your reproductive organs and glands.

- Tunes up your nervous system naturally and efficiently.

For women, there are some contraindications for the Stretch Pose, considering that this kriya puts extra pressure on the reproductive system. Therefore, women have to take care of:

- Pregnant women should not do this, especially those who have crossed 120 days of pregnancy.

- Women with pregnancy complications should avoid doing this pose. Speak to a qualified instructor for modifications or help.

- Women experiencing the first few heavy-bleeding days of the menstrual cycle should not do this kriya.

The Stretch Pose can be done using these steps:

- Lie on your back comfortably on a blanket or sheet made of natural fiber.

- Raise your head and your heels about six inches above the ground.

- Stretch your toes away from you.

- Focus your eyes on the tips of your toes.

- Place your hands above your thighs (or legs, if you can lift yourself to that extent), ensuring they don't touch. The palms of your hands must face downward.

- Do the Breath of Fire.

Ideally, hold this position for 1-3 minutes (yes, challenging indeed). Usually, most people can hold this position for not over 30 seconds, during which you can feel the pull of your muscles. After this, your body might shake, and your face could become contorted because of the pressure on the muscles. Beginners are definitely not expected to hold this position for the entire duration. For beginners, holding for three minutes is almost impossible. Use these techniques to slowly build strength and confidence in your abilities:

Place your hands behind your back and under your buttocks, palms facing downwards. This position gives strength and support to your lower back and allows you to keep your legs raised more easily than otherwise.

Raise one leg at a time instead of both together. Hold the position with your right leg raised and your left leg firmly fixed to the ground.

Then switch your leg positions. The leg placed on the ground will enhance your stability, facilitating your ability to hold the other leg in a raised position for a longer time.

Alternately, you could raise both your legs simultaneously but keep your knees slightly bent. This will also reduce the difficulty of doing the kriya in the initial states.

Another way to build stamina for this exercise is to alternate holding the pose and resting for 10 seconds each. Gradually you can increase the duration until you can keep the position for longer periods.

Start small and gradually increase your ability to enhance the time of holding the Stretch Pose.

Stamina and Vitality Building Kriya

This kriya unleashes the powerful inner energy lying latent within you so you can harness the power of increased stamina and vitality. This kriya starts its magic by releasing the stored energy from the navel point and taking this energy to all the major and minor nadis of your body.

Then, this kriya drives the energy up from the solar plexus chakra to the throat chakra to energize the higher glands there. Finally, the Sushumna is cleared of all the blockages, and the energy is released into this superhighway Nadi. It is a great kriya for beginners and the experienced practitioners of Kundalini Yoga.

Bend at your hip and balance your body on the tips of your toes and fingertips. Keep your knees straight but not locked uncomfortably.

In this position, move your hips rapidly. Imagine how an animal would swish its tail. Replicate that move rapidly. Do this for three minutes.

Next, sit in the easy pose and push your spine back at a 60-degree angle. Your arms should be folded in front of you. Keep your neck straight. Now, roll your shoulders in a forward circle. This exercise also has to be done for three minutes.

Lie down in the baby pose. Interlock your fingers by bringing your hands to the small of your back. Now, raise your arms over your back in a yoga pose and keep this position for three minutes.

Next, sit cross-legged on the floor in lotus pose and lean back by supporting yourself on your elbows. Hold this position for three minutes.

Next, sit on the floor and stretch out your legs. Now, touch your toes and bring your head to touch your knees and come back up. Do this movement not over 11 times rapidly. Remember to breathe normally and NOT use the breath of fire technique.

The last pose requires you to sit in Sukhasana. With the Pranam Mudra, focus your eyes on the tip of your nose. Keep your neck straight and your chest and chin out. Pump your navel point, imagining a million points of light emerging from there and filling your body with its energy. Do this for 3 minutes.

To end the kriya, inhale deeply and hold. In this position, tighten all the muscles in your body. After about 10 seconds, exhale explosively out of your mouth. Repeat this breathing technique twice more. Slowly open your eyes.

Kriya to Conquer and Overcome Pain

The self-healing kriya helps you conquer and overcome pain by balancing your central nervous system. It trains your body to conquer pain, which will help you overcome any problem in your life.

Sit in an easy pose keeping your spine erect and relaxed.

Split your fingers so your middle and index fingers are touching each other, and the little and ring fingers are touching each other. Stretch your arms sideways and parallel to the ground. In this position, you will feel a stretch in your armpit. The palm of your left hand should face downward, and that of your right hand should face upward.

Now, inhale through the mouth and breathe out through the nostrils. Slow your breathing as much as you can until you can complete only three breathing cycles per minute. Ensure your arms are straight, and you feel the stretch in your armpits. This kriya has to be done for 11 minutes.

To end the kriya, inhale deeply through your mouth, hold your breath, making sure your arms are fully stretched outwards, and your spine is stretched upwards. Then exhale through your nose. Repeat this breathing sequence twice more before you slowly open your eyes.

Detoxification Kriya

Humans have evolved to take in more than we can process. For example, frequently, we eat more than our daily requirements accumulating the unprocessed food in our body. We accumulate a lot of negative emotions and experiences, unwittingly, and wittingly. Therefore, often, we feel bogged down by the negativities and the unprocessed excess we have accumulated in our life.

Precious energy is often utilized to take care of these unproductive accumulations. Detoxifying ourselves will not only help in getting rid of physical, emotional, and mental toxins but also help us conserve precious energy to be used for productive purposes. Therefore, we need to continuously detoxify our mind and body to keep us light, healthy, and flexible. The detoxifying kriya is designed specifically for this purpose.

1. Lie down on your back. Your heels should be straight, together and touching the ground, and your toes should be pointed upward.

Now, spread your feet apart so the right foot points to the right and the left foot to the left.

Next, bring your feet together so they are pointing upward again. Continue this opening and closing of your feet for four minutes.

2. Remain lying on your back. Put your hands behind your head.

Raise your legs about two feet and do the scissoring action with them, ensuring your heels do not touch the floor.

3. Keep your legs straight and knees unbent. Do this exercise for four minutes.

Next, lie on your stomach. Breathe out through your mouth as you raise the top portion of your body in the cobra pose.

Inhale through your mouth as you lower your body back to the ground. This exercise is excellent for getting rid of toxins from your body. Do it for about six minutes.

4. Next, lie down on your back again. Bring your knees up to your chest.

Raise your arms upward at a 90-degree angle.

Straighten your knees and lower your hands back to the ground.

Do this exercise for three minutes, ensuring your movements are controlled. There should be no sound as your hands and legs are lowered to the back.

5. Sit in the easy pose. Now, revolve your torso in the counterclockwise direction around the base of your backbone like a churning motion.

Do this exercise for three minutes, trying to increase the speed of revolution in the last minute.

6. Next, stand up straight. Bend forward and hold or grab your ankles. Sit in a crow pose as you hold your ankle. Now, come back up. Do this exercise for two minutes.

You can end this kriya by sitting in an easy pose and chanting the Sat Nam Mantra for 11 minutes. After the meditation, stretch your arms above your head with your palms touching each other. Inhale as you do this and hold your breath for 20-40 seconds, depending on your ability. Slowly exhale. Repeat this breathing sequence twice more before you open your eyes.

The kriyas will take time and effort to master. Achieving the maximum recommended duration for each kriya will not happen for beginners. Start small and gradually increase your intensity and duration for each kriya until you can do it for the entire maximum recommended period. To reiterate, do not try to do for more than the maximum recommended time. Follow the steps strictly for optimal benefits.

Chapter 9: Tantra and Other Practices

Practicing the Kundalini Yoga through asanas, pranayama, kriyas, mudras and meditations is an excellent way to awaken the Kundalini; you need to do more than spending a few minutes dedicated to this exercise. You must include the practice of Kundalini Awakening into your daily routine.

The desire to awaken the Kundalini should be part of your life's purpose. Also, there are multiple ways of including daily habits, changing your lifestyle, and altering your mindset that will help you to build your strength and capability to awaken the dormant but powerful serpent within you. When you have mastered the basics, then advanced options like Shaktipat and Tantra can take you further ahead in your journey.

Everyday Techniques to Awaken Your Kundalini

Focus on your breathing - Any exercise that drives you to focus on your breath is helpful for Kundalini Awakening. So, learn to live a more mindful lifestyle. Focus on the present moment. Regardless of the task you do, try to notice how your breath comes and goes.

The best and the most effective method of focusing on your breath is to spend just five minutes each day noticing your breathing. Do the simple breathing exercise explained in an earlier chapter. Even if you do nothing else, this simple breathing exercise will get you closer to your goal of Kundalini Awakening.

If you have a problem remembering to do it, set the alarm after or before your lunch break and just before your bedtime. Do five minutes of breathing exercises sitting anywhere comfortable and undisturbed.

Avoid negativity of all kinds in your life - The more positive you are, the more positivity you will attract. The reverse is also true, which means to say that the more positivity you bring into your life, the more positive you will become. One way to attract positivity is by rejecting negativity.

Notice all the negative patterns in your life. It could be in the way you think, in the company you keep, and your overall general perspective. As and when you come across negativity in any aspect of your life, either eliminate it or replace it with something good. The second way of managing negativity is called rephrasing or reframing. Each time you catch yourself thinking negatively, reword the situation or thought into something positive.

For example, what if you planned on going out for lunch with your friends on a Saturday afternoon, and suddenly it rained cats and dogs? Instead of getting angry about the weather, you could tell yourself, 'this is a great opportunity to finish that painting I have been putting off."

Here is another example of reframing thoughts positively. Suppose you got a rejection letter from a company you applied for a job. Instead of telling yourself that you didn't get it because you were not worthy of the offer, tell yourself that you didn't get it because something much better is right around the corner.

Use visualization techniques - Visualization exercises are powerful tools to enhance all the right things in your life, including the journey of Kundalini Awakening. Visualize the divine light sparked at the base of your spine and slowly rising up and moving toward the crown. Visualize this bright light spreading warmth and the light of knowledge and wisdom to every cell in your body. As you visualize, repeat these affirmation statements:

Divine light is my source of energy.

Divine light creates me and expands my knowledge and wisdom.

Divine light protects me.

I am bathed in this divine light.

Activate your interests and hobbies - Activating your interests and hobbies is not just good for awakening your Kundalini but is also useful toward leading a happy and balanced life. But to awaken your Kundalini, it is imperative you spend at least an hour each day investing time and energy on an activity that keeps you not just happy but engaged and immersed.

The challenge with this point is that our hectic lives and societal pressures drive us to invest time and energy only on "productive" tasks, and hobbies and interests which have no monetary value are seen to be treated as "unproductive." It is time to change this attitude and fight against this approach.

List things you are dying to do but unable to because of the lack of time and energy. Make another list of things you are compelled to do because they are more productive, even if they don't make you happy. Replace unhappy activities with happy ones and see the difference this choice will make in your life and life experiences. Joyful living is a critical aspect of Kundalini Awakening.

Yogic Daily Habits for Kundalini Awakening

As you practice Kundalini Yoga, the increased awareness impacts all aspects of your life ranging from the mundane daily activities to the more esoteric philosophical thinking process you are likely to imbibe during your journey. This section is dedicated to showing you how to change your daily activities with increased awareness so they, too, contribute to the process of Kundalini Awakening. These habits, simple and ordinary as they may seem, have a huge impact on our vitality and consciousness.

Brushing your teeth - Thanks to your dentist, you already know the importance of brushing your teeth for the health of your teeth, mouth and gums. Now, learn how an awareness-rich habit of brushing your teeth will positively affect your Kundalini Awakening process.

At night, as you sleep, your mouth becomes an incubator in which hundreds and thousands of bacteria grow and develop. The best places for these bacteria to thrive are two small pockets in your throat. Therefore, if you don't brush your teeth and cleanse your mouth right up to the back of your tongue, the chances of swallowing these disease-causing bacteria increase significantly.

As soon as you get up in the morning, brush your teeth well and then use your toothbrush to cleanse up to the back of the tongue so deeply that you gag, which is a good thing. With this gagging, all the bacteria are thrown out of your mouth, and your mouth, tongue, teeth and throat are ready to face the world.

As you gag out the bacteria, your eyes will water, which is another good thing because these tears will help in preserving eyesight. The toothpowder to use for cleaning your tongue and to induce gagging can be made of these ingredients: 1 part sea salt and 2 parts potassium alum.

You can make this powder and store it in a jar in your bathroom. Put a little every day in the palm of your hand. Then, wash your toothbrush and dip it in the powder and brush your teeth and tongue. You can complete brushing your teeth with your favorite toothpaste.

Importance of sleep for Kundalini Awakening - Sleep is essential to rest your body and mind so they can recuperate and rejuvenate. Only after a restful sleep can you feel alert to face the challenges of a new day. Here are tips as to how you should prepare your sleeping space to ensure you get a restful night's sleep every day.

- Your mattress should be firm enough to support your spine and allow your nervous system to relax.

- Let your bed be aligned along with east-west direction for a peaceful night's sleep. If your bed is in the same direction as the Earth's magnetic field (north-south direction), then your personal energy could get overpowered, resulting in quality-compromised sleep. You will wake up grouchy and tired.

- See if you can have inspirational music or affirmations playing gently in the background in your bedroom, especially before your bedtime. You can keep this sound playing at almost inaudible levels so it flows directly into your subconscious mind.

Here are useful tips to prepare for sleep:

- You should have sweated and laughed out your daily quota before your bedtime. If you haven't, then go for a walk before you lie down to sleep.

- Do not have heavy night-time meals.

- Brush your teeth before sleeping.

- Drink a glass of water, if you want. Dehydration at night can cause disturbed sleep. Getting up to go to the bathroom will not disturb it. You can get back and fall asleep again easily.

- Just before lying down on your bed, wash your feet with cold water. This helps to calm down and relax your nervous system.

- Meditate or say your prayers.

Helpful tips to fall asleep:

- Take all your worries and problems. Pack them in a suitcase. Lock it and put them on a shelf that reads GOD. You will be amazed at how this simple visualization exercise can help calm down your nerves.

- Set the alarm in your mind to wake up when you want to. Yes, you don't need an outside alarm. The subconscious mind keeps excellent time and will respond to your order.

- Lie on your stomach with your right cheek on the pillow. This position will ensure your left nostril is open to breathe in calming, soothing energy. In this position, do long breathing exercises with both your nostrils.

- Once you feel sleepy, then turn over and sleep in your preferred position.

Hydrotherapy in Kundalini Yoga

One of the most important morning habits that promises good health is a cold shower. The process, cruel as it might seem, is a powerful tool called hydrotherapy or "ishnaan." A cold shower goes beyond keeping your physical and external body clean and hygienic. The benefits of hydrotherapy are multifold.

- When the cold water hits your skin, all the blood rushes to your organs. This movement of blood-flow toward the organs is a way of protecting the organs and will keep them warm against the hit of cold water. It is an innate self-defense mechanism of our body.

- As the blood rushes inward towards the various organs, the blood capillaries are flushed out, resulting in a powerful workout for them. Cold showers clear blood vessels and flush out the toxins.

- Also, the circulation system is vastly benefited from a cold shower, leaving your skin and blood cells rejuvenated and refreshed. A cold shower also stimulates increased secretions in the glandular system, resulting in the improved working of your body and mind.

Helpful tips to have a cold shower each morning:

- Massage your entire body with small amount of almond oil before the shower. It contains a lot of minerals and does not stick to the body. When wet, almond oil gets easily absorbed by your skin.

- Wear cotton boxers or shorts to cover your thighs to protect your femur bone from the direct impact of the cold water.

- Open the cold shower. Get under and out of the shower several times, continuously massaging your body until the water doesn't feel cold anymore. Yes, when you repeatedly get in and out of the cold shower, your skin and body will get accustomed to the coldness and will not send jumpy signals to your brain.

- Start with your lower limbs, then move to your arms, and when you are ready, get your whole body under the shower.

If you have a problem with sciatica or high blood pressure, check with your doctor before you try this therapy.

Special tips for women:

- Ensure you massage your breasts to release toxins and improve circulation.

- Avoid cold showers when menstruating.

- If you are pregnant, your baby should not be under the cold water for over three minutes. And after the seventh month, do not have cold water showers. Again, speak to your doctor before trying hydrotherapy if you are pregnant.

- After the shower, dry off your body briskly. This will give your body a good shine.

Advanced Methods of Awakening the Kundalini

Once you have learned and mastered the basics, you can move on to advanced methods that help to awaken your Kundalini. Two of the most popular and accepted advanced include Tantra and Shaktipat. Let us look in briefly at each element.

Tantra - A lot of confusion exists for understanding Tantra, essential esoteric traditions connected to both Hinduism and Buddhism. Sadly, in the western world, the uninitiated look at Tantra as a means of sexual empowerment. Tantra goes beyond and above materialistic sexual empowerment.

There are advanced mantra meditation techniques in Tantra used to awaken the Kundalini. A famous Tantric scripture called Vijñāna Bhairava Tantra lists 112 tantric meditation techniques. Another tantric school called Bhairavanand Tantra is derived from Shaivism and teaches practitioners advanced lessons using mantra meditation to awaken the Kundalini. And this tradition uses a combination of yantras and yagnas.

Yantras are special geometric shapes known to have the power to affect tangible changes at the physical level by energy from subtler energy levels. Yagnas are large sacrificial fires over which mantras are chanted along with sacred elements submitted to the fire to achieve special wishes.

Shaktipat - Shaktipat is the transfer of spiritual energy from a guru to a well-prepared and deserving student. This energy transfer mechanism not only results in new energy being received by the student but also enhancing and conserving his or her own energy.

Transferring energy through Shaktipat happens in many ways, including through touch, use of a mantra, or sometimes merely by sight. Interestingly, the guru might not necessarily be transferring his or her own energy, but the energy from the ancient and past gurus from their lineage.

Students view Shaktipat as a form of grace by their guru, and therefore, is difficult to achieve. Your guru should be truly pleased with your efforts to awaken the Kundalini, and you must be prepared to take on the challenges that come with the energy of the awakened serpent.

There are other ways of awakening the Kundalini including through sex too. Yes, our biological instincts can prove to be the gateway for spiritual awakening. Energies of the two partners can resonate during lovemaking leading to an increased spiritual experience that affects both the partners simultaneously.

And yet, it is important to know that the awakening of your Kundalini is an uncontrollable and spontaneous event. If you find your Kundalini awakened, it is out of your control. You can only persist and wait patiently for the moment when it happens. Different life experiences might drive this energy to move up the spine without or without your knowledge.

And yes, someone who has been practicing for years in Kundalini Yoga might not succeed yet, whereas someone who has never heard of this concept might experience it, unwittingly, of course.

Chapter 10: What to Do After a Kundalini Awakening

Let us assume you have had your Kundalini Awakening. Now, what do you do? What to expect when this momentous time comes? How to handle yourself and your life after it? This chapter is dedicated to these aspects.

First things first. When you experience Kundalini Awakening, you will definitely feel scared, disoriented, and quite awful. Often, the awakening of the Kundalini might seem like a mental illness or a mesh of emotional difficulties that seem insurmountable to the new and the uninitiated.

It can be quite difficult to get your bearings, even if you have been waiting for this day for years. All you will know is that something really freaky is happening to you. In fact, there are stories of real-life cases where people who have had Kundalini Awakenings have not been able to deal with it and have been institutionalized and even addicted to drugs driven by fears and insecurities.

Benefits and Changes to expect with Kundalini Awakening

An increased range of emotions and feelings - One of the first things you will experience with a Kundalini Awakening is that your range of emotions, both intensity and number, will increase significantly. So, you will find yourself able to feel even the subtlest emotions in your mind. For example, if you are in a crowded area, you could hear the sobs of someone crying in pain somewhere in the crowd that no one else there had noticed. The spectrum of your emotional experience will increase multifold.

Also, you will feel energetically sensitive. As you walk on the road, you unwittingly absorb all kinds of emotional energies. This experience can be very unsettling, considering that the emotions you absorb are not limited to the positive ones. These feelings are not really yours but other people's, and yet, you will feel deeply connected to these emotions. Yes, that will unsettle you for a while until you have learned how to draw healthy boundaries and learn to handle the newfound talent.

Your life will change forever - The awakening of the Kundalini is going to teach you lessons you never dreamed of. The energy levels in your body, mind, and spirit will increase to unimaginable levels. Your life after the awakening is going to be very different from what it was before. And therein lies the difficulty of coping, especially in the initial days.

Be prepared for a tremendous change as you find the law of attraction working in more direct ways than before. You will find the universe fulfilling your needs even as you think about it. Your ability to discern and follow your life purpose will get a huge boost. Life will support you at every step of the way.

You find yourself closer to the universal divine being - One reason why life will never be the same is that you find yourself close to the universal divine being whom we call God, Shiva, or by any other name. You will feel and experience the closeness with the divine spirit, and your earlier misbeliefs about the Supreme Being will melt into nothingness.

The biggest benefit of Kundalini Awakening is that you will learn there is far, far more to life than birth, surviving your lifetime, and then dying. You will see you are nothing more than a speck in this mighty vast universe. Yet, you will feel a distinct and deep connection knowing you are from that same root.

Suggestions to Overcome Challenges of Kundalini Awakening

Identify, accept, and embrace what is happening to you - This is the foremost and yet one of the most difficult steps to take when your Kundalini is awakened, and you feel strange and unfamiliar with everything happening in your life. The biggest hit you will get with the rising of the Kundalini is your ego will be shattered to bits.

While it is a great thing to happen, in the initial stages, not having an ego will create problems because you have never had to live without it. Therefore, functioning normally in society will be compromised. In fact, people with such experiences are known to have quit their jobs because they couldn't take what was happening.

Also, your heightened sensitivity to light, sounds, and all sensations can drive you insane. The perception filters you had earlier can all disappear, and it can be a scary experience initially and until you come to terms with it.

Remind yourself not to fight this strange experience. Embrace it and allow yourself to experience the strangeness and unfamiliarity fully and completely. Find your own ways to embrace the new life. Only when you embrace it can you use the powers that come with Kundalini Awakening effectively and sensibly.

Seek professional help - This is an important first step you should take. If you are already learning Kundalini Yoga from a guru or instructor, then you must contact him or her when you feel weird or experience unfamiliar things in your life. If you are trying something on your own and you have problems, then find a local guide or mentor to help you out.

If you live in a remote part of the world, then try to find someone through the Internet. From a spiritual perspective, awakening the Kundalini is like waking up an unknown part of your soul, and you don't know what to expect. Therefore, sometimes, a religious guide like a rabbi or a priest might help.

The trick is in finding someone who understands this core aspect of human experience and will guide you through the strange and difficult experiences.

Seek professional help for your physical, mental and emotional effects too - Spiritually, you could be blissed out and on cloud nine. In this state, you tend to ignore your physical, mental and emotional aspects of your life, considering that you will be totally caught up in the whirlpool of your Kundalini Awakening episode.

For your physical needs, find a doctor who understands the mind-body connection and knows what kind of diagnostic tools he or she must use to keep your body in physical well-being. If you find yourself being mentally unstable, seek the help of a professional therapist in the psychology and/or psychiatry field. This professional should also be able to understand there are aspects of the human world that go beyond the subtle mind.

Sometimes, even drugs might be needed to be prescribed to help you overcome the difficulties arising from certain experiences. A practical approach to the experience of Kundalini Awakening is critical. Know that you are likely to be in some above-human realm, and with all the reading you have done about Kundalini Awakening, remind yourself to remain grounded even in such a state and seek help from people who can assist you harness the unleashed power sensibly.

Get mental clarity and keep yourself grounded - With the help of professionals, make sure you have mental clarity in and about what is going on in your life. A Kundalini Awakening has its roots in spirituality but affects everything in our lives. Your DNA gets rewired so your body and mind get increased capabilities to handle the extra flow of prana that is an automatic outcome of Kundalini Awakening. Therefore, you need to have an immense amount of mental clarity to handle your life.

Stop consuming alcohol completely and other intoxicants completely. If you are into drugs, that has to stop immediately. Otherwise, you are risking your sanity. Even the food you eat must get your attention. Get rid of all kinds of processed foods. Include lean meats, root vegetables and fruit and nuts to help you get grounded.

Ensure you get your regular exercise. Connecting physically with the earth element through physical workouts is a great way to ground yourself. Take care of your physical health is the basis of keeping yourself grounded and your mind clear and prepared to handle the huge energy uptake that comes with Kundalini Awakening.

Connect with like-minded people - Having a group of people with whom you can talk about your experiences is a great way to help you manage the difficult time. There are a lot of support groups you can find online. Join a group and discuss your problems with them. Even if you are unsure about talking with newly founded friends about your strange experiences, you can listen in to their experiences and connect with them.

Speaking to others who think like you will help you understand that you are not alone in this world. There are others who are ahead of you in the field, and there are others trying to catch up. This knowledge gives you a deep sense of belonging to a community bound by a common goal. Sharing each other's experiences will be a huge help.

Also, finding professional help in such groups is easy too. Someone or other will have already set a path in this direction. You will just have to follow it.

Get a daily practice routine in place - If you don't already have a daily practice of Kundalini Yoga, then start one right away. Daily practice of kriyas is a great way to keep yourself grounded and also increase your ability to handle the newly opened channels of energy sensibly and well. It might be a good idea to avoid meditation in the initial days of Kundalini Awakening because it can get intense, and you could be in a position in which the power of energy release is higher than your ability to handle it.

Yoga Asanas and kriyas are great. Also, include journaling every day, making sure all your experiences are documented. Journaling is not only an excellent method to create a reference for future use but also a way of getting your nagging and fearful thoughts out of your head, at least for a while.

Don't stop learning about Kundalini - The subject is vast and limitless. The more you learn, the more newer information you will get. Not only this, but you can also interpret old knowledge in new ways, allowing you to handle issues in innovative methods as you include these new lessons into your life.

Remind yourself that your experience is new and special to you. However, you are not unique. You are not one of a kind. The Kundalini serpent is lying dormant in all humans. You have had the fortune to learn about it and awaken its power. There have been people before you who did this, and there will be others who will do it in the future too.

These humbling reminders are excellent grounding factors and also prevent you from having grandiose ideas and thoughts about yourself. When you are practical and realistic about the experiences connected to Kundalini Awakening, your ability to harness its powers usefully, productively and wisely will improve significantly.

The experience of a Kundalini Awakening is painful and agonizing but highly rewarding in all respects. Your entire life will see and feel its positive benefits as you live your life more meaningfully and more deeply connected with the universe than before. The people around you will be impacted positively as they get attracted to and learn from the increased aura around you.

The will of the divine cannot really be suppressed. The more you run away from your life, the harder it will chase you. Therefore, regardless of the pain and difficulties that come your way, embracing life as it comes to you is the best and most effective way to live. If you have been driven to read up and learn about Kundalini, then this part of your life will inevitably take place. It might take longer than you thought. It might be more difficult than you thought. But the experience will happen because you are karmically designed to experience the Kundalini Awakening.

Conclusion

The universe is only a limitless expanse of energy. Your life is a bundle of energy too. Everything we do, say or perform and every interaction with others, etc. are all different forms of energy. Kundalini Yoga is designed to awaken the dormant Kundalini energy within you. Once awakened (in the right way and at its own pace), the power harnessed from the Kundalini can have huge positive impacts on all aspects of your life.

Remember that your trials and tribulations of life will not go away when you awaken your Kundalini. However, this awakened energy will guide you perfectly through all your problems, ensuring you have not just a smooth ride but also a deeply meaningful and fulfilling life.

However, it might happen at the most unexpected of times because it is not under your control. Even now, you could have doubts like, "I have been trying to awaken it for years, and nothing seems to be happening." For some people, energy blockages could be cleared with a simple exercise, whereas for others, more complex and persistent effort might be needed.

We have multiple subtle bodies, and the Kundalini has to pass through them all to rise up and allow you to feel its full impact.

Sometimes, by chance, the Kundalini might appear to have opened up. However, such superficial awakenings can never do the full job.

Therefore, remember to persist, and your patience will be rewarded. The interesting thing is that the reward can never be explained fully by anyone. What you feel and experience when your Kundalini awakens is yours alone. All the theories you read will go straight out of the window when this experience hits you personally. One of the most important lessons to learn when it comes to beyond-realm theories and practices is that you can realize the lessons only when you experience it yourself. That is the only way.

Here's another book by Mari Silva that you might like

References

https://www.ramdass.org/shakti-prana/

https://www.youtube.com/watch?v=7DWkY78wp7c

https://www.ananda.org/ask/is-there-a-difference-between-kundalini-energy-and-prana

https://karaleah.com/2018/10/what-is-a-kundalini-awakening-and-have-i-had-one

https://www.chakras.info/kundalini/

https://karaleah.com/2018/10/kundalini-awakenings-symptoms-process-benefits-support-help/

https://thoughtcatalog.com/brianna-wiest/2018/08/16-signs-youre-having-whats-known-as-a-kundalini-awakening/

https://www.youtube.com/watch?v=G22hZ81Vku0

https://www.youtube.com/watch?v=mMMerxh_12U

https://www.verywellmind.com/what-is-kundalini-meditation-4688618

https://chopra.com/articles/the-root-chakra-muladhara

https://iarp.org/chakra-basics/

https://www.watkinspublishing.com/working-with-your-chakras-swami-saradananda/

https://www.thebluebudha.com.au/the-sixth-third-eye-chakra-our-sixth-sense-our-psychic-powers/

https://www.jackcanfield.com/blog/cultivating-intuition/

https://www.lifehack.org/articles/productivity/10-ways-nurture-your-creativity-and-boost-your-intuitive-awareness.html

https://www.chakras.info/opening-third-eye

https://www.kundaliniyoga.org/Asanas

https://www.3ho.org/3ho-lifestyle/women/kundalini-yoga-woman-s-set

https://www.3ho.org/kundalini-yoga/pranayam/pranayam-techniques

https://www.youtube.com/watch?v=MhPqAh69Gmw,

https://www.youtube.com/watch?v=e5tGCr22TlA

https://www.3ho.org/kundalini-yoga/mantra/kundalini-yoga-mantras

https://www.3ho.org/kundalini-yoga/mudra

https://www.youtube.com/watch?v=QaVzpbias4Y

https://www.youtube.com/watch?v=nCPj98L979w

https://www.thelawofattraction.com/awaken-kundalini/

https://www.3ho.org/3ho-lifestyle/daily-routine

https://karaleah.com/2018/10/suggestions-on-what-to-do-if-youve-had-a-kundalini-awakening/

https://www.youtube.com/watch?v=1P0k1ZC9gkc

CPSIA information can be obtained
at www.ICGtesting.com
Printed in the USA
BVHW030910211021
619525BV00002B/48